GREAT CYCLE ROUTES

HAMPSHIRE & DORSET

JOHN PRICE

First published 2001

ISBN 0 7110 2779 X

Published by Dial House

an imprint of Ian Allan Publishing Ltd, Hersham, Surrey KT12 4RG.
Printed by Ian Allan Printing Ltd, Hersham, Surrey KT12 4RG.

Code: 0104/D

Front cover:
The thatched barns and abbey at Abbotsbury and (inset) enjoying the ride near Tarrant Gunville.

Title page:
Hampshire signposts are quaint but ineffective.

This page:
Cyclists on the Meon Valley cycleway.

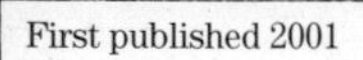

First published 2001

ISBN 0 7110 2779 X

Published by Dial House

an imprint of Ian Allan Publishing Ltd, Hersham, Surrey KT12 4RG.
Printed by Ian Allan Printing Ltd, Hersham, Surrey KT12 4RG.

Code: 0104/D

Front cover:
The thatched barns and abbey at Abbotsbury and (inset) enjoying the ride near Tarrant Gunville.

Title page:
Hampshire signposts are quaint but ineffective.

This page:
Cyclists on the Meon Valley cycleway.

CONTENTS

INTRODUCTION

INTRODUCTION

I must make it clear right from the start that this book is written for 'potterers' who wish to take their time exploring, enjoying and discovering the countryside at no particular pace. It is not a book for lycra-clad athletes with full-suspension machines who try to cover the roughest and steepest terrain in the shortest possible time. It is written with families in mind, who may either live in or near one of the two counties, or are intending to take a holiday there. The book describes 30 rides in detail covering over 520 miles of cycling mainly on quiet country lanes but also on old railway lines, canal towpaths, and through forests. It provides background information on places of interest on the rides or nearby, and in addition it contains a wealth of material on all the cycling opportunities in the area, with the addresses of organisations who can provide further information.

Wherever possible, extensive use has been made of river valleys as they usually offer scenic routes with much interest and, above all, they provide cycling with the hills taken out. But no book of cycle rides in Hampshire or Dorset can completely avoid hills, especially with the topography ranging from flat sandy heathland to chalk downland approaching 300m, so I would not wish the reader to think that there will be no hills to keep him or her fit and healthy!

Having cycled all of these miles, approximately equally divided between Hampshire and Dorset, I became aware of the small but fascinating differences between the two counties. If you were blindfolded and placed in the middle of Dorset, the first thing that you would notice, when the blindfold was removed, would be the peculiar quaintness of the place names. Toller Porcorum, Childe Okeford, Sixpenny Handley, Ryme Intrinseca and Tarrant Gunville are my particular favourites, but there are many others that are equally characteristic of the county. If the same blindfold exercise were conducted in Hampshire, it would be the signposts that would give the game away. Signposts in rural Hampshire are quirky, and there seems to be no standard design. You will often find at a junction that there is no signpost at all. This type of unmarked junction occurs when you are totally lost and at a point when you would find a friendly signpost really helpful. When signposts (usually leaning) are provided at junctions, these are often less than useful and fall into two distinct types. The first is where just one direction is given and invariably this tells you where you have just come from. The second is where full signposting is provided. Initially this is quite impressive until you look a little closer and find that the 'fingers' are not secured to the pole and are free to swing around in the wind. Signposting in Dorset is a complete contrast. The signposts are virtually all made to a standard pattern. They are robust, reliable and not only have the junction name clearly shown, but they also show the national six-figure grid reference as well.

Cycling these routes throughout the summer of 2000 has left me with some very pleasant memories, and with just one worry. You will realise from using this book that one of the great pleasures of a cycle ride in southern England is to stop off for refreshment at a country pub. There are signs that this is going to become increasingly difficult as significant numbers are closing. Several times I designed a ride, based on Ordnance Survey information, and expected to find a pub at a chosen spot for lunch, only to discover that it had been converted into a private residence. According to CAMRA about 20 pubs a month are closing. It is a common practice in rural areas for unscrupulous pub owners to run down a business, delicence the pub and sell it off at a large profit as a private house. Let us hope that this trend is reversed, or one of the unique qualities of rural England will disappear.

Finally, cycling is one of the few activities that almost all members of the family can enjoy together irrespective of age. So if today is a fine day and you find yourself with some spare time in Hampshire or Dorset, choose your route, oil that chain and get cycling. You will feel better for it!

Key to Directions

Each instruction is of the following type:

'7. (8.9 miles): At the junction with the sealed road, turn right . . .'

This means at Point No 7 on the sketch map, at a distance of 8.9 miles you should follow the stated instruction. Directions are given only

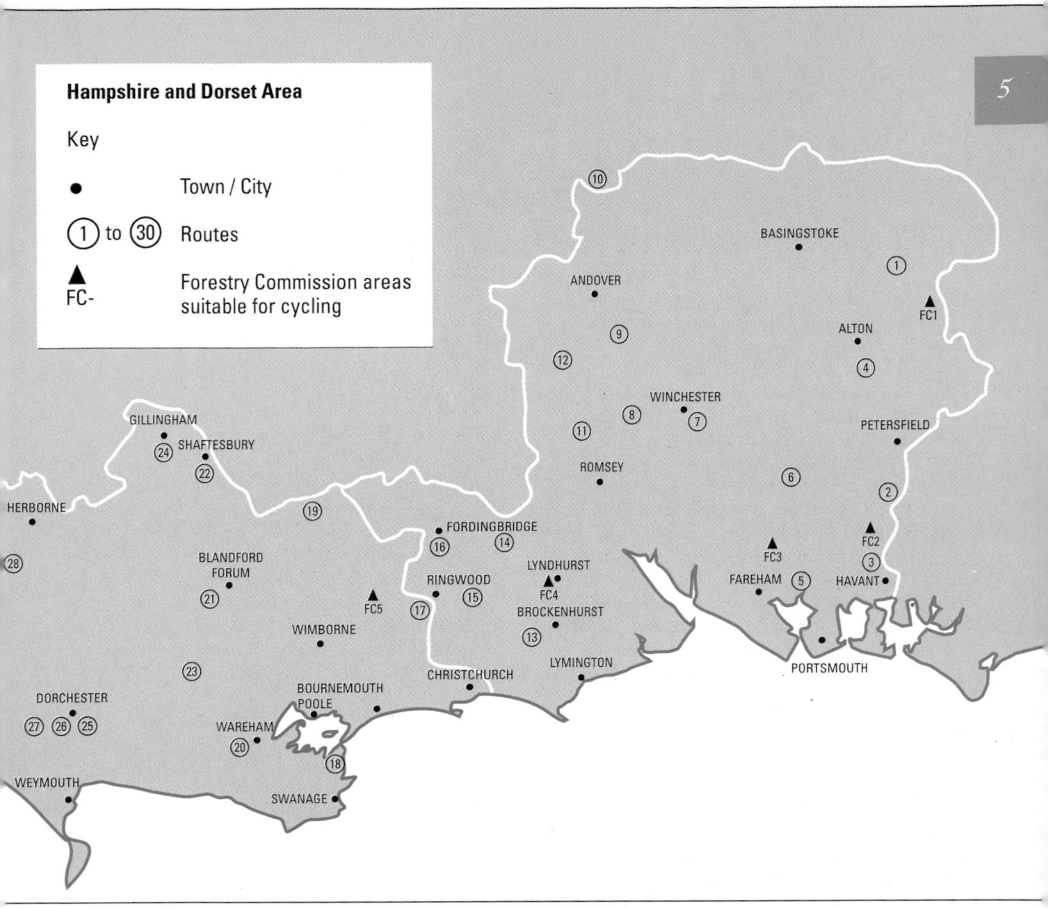

Hampshire and Dorset Area

Key

● Town / City

(1) to (30) Routes

▲ FC- Forestry Commission areas suitable for cycling

BASINGSTOKE (1) ANDOVER FC1 ALTON (9) (12) (4) WINCHESTER (8) (7) PETERSFIELD (11) ROMSEY (6) (2) GILLINGHAM SHAFTESBURY (24) (22) HERBORNE (19) FORDINGBRIDGE (16) (14) FC2 FC3 (28) BLANDFORD FORUM LYNDHURST FAREHAM (5) (3) HAVANT RINGWOOD (15) FC4 (21) FC5 (17) BROCKENHURST WIMBORNE (13) LYMINGTON PORTSMOUTH (23) CHRISTCHURCH BOURNEMOUTH DORCHESTER POOLE (27) (26) (25) WAREHAM (20) (18) WEYMOUTH SWANAGE

where you will need to deviate from the most obvious route, or if some confusion could occur. If no instructions are given at a particular place, keep straight on.

ACKNOWLEDGEMENTS
On a personal note I would like to thank my wife Veronica for her considerable contribution with background research and for her company on many rides. Also I would like to thank my son Christopher and his family, who also accompanied me on some rides and agreed to be photographed for the book.

I am grateful to Roger Porch who checked the section on the use of the railways for getting to the rides, and to Colin Palmer and Michael Seddon of the Forestry Commission who provided information on Forestry Commission cycling opportunities.

Picture Credits
All uncredited photographs are by the author. Maps are by RS Illustrations, Liss, Hants.

BACKGROUND SOURCES
The author wishes to mention the following sources as having been particularly valuable for reference and background: *The AA Book of British Villages* (Drive Publications Ltd); *The Hampshire Village Book*, by Anthony Brode (Countryside Books); *The Hidden Places of Hampshire and the Isle of Wight*, by Joy David (M&M Publishing Ltd); *Hampshire Customs, Curiosities & Country Lore*, by John Edgar Mann (Ensign Publications); *Arthur Mee's The King's England — Dorset* (Hodder and Stoughton); *Highways and Byways in Hampshire*, by D. H. Moutray Read (Macmillan & Co); *Highways and Byways in Dorset*, by Sir Frederick Treves (Macmillan and Co); *www.thedorsetpage.com.*

WHERE TO CYCLE

The aim of this book is to supply the ideas and information that a family needs to enjoy a day of safe cycling in Hampshire and Dorset. Information has been obtained from many sources including Sustrans, the Cyclists' Touring Club, Dorset and Hampshire County Councils, the Forestry Commission, the Basingstoke Canal Authority and others. The book is aimed at the family, who have children of cycling age, that either live in Hampshire or Dorset, or alternatively are having a holiday there.

CYCLING ON QUIET ROADS

Although cycling on traffic-free routes is the safest form of cycling, I often prefer to cycle on quiet country roads as they are more likely to take you through our beautiful villages, which a railway or canal-based route might very well bypass. Obviously it is important to select the route carefully, so that 'rat-runs' can be avoided and the number of crossings of busy main roads minimised. One tell-tale sign of a country road that is good for cycling is one that has some weed growth in the middle. This growth is due to lack of vehicular traffic and these are usually delightfully quiet. Another sign of a road that is suitable for quiet cycling is one that has been incorporated into a county council cycleway, the National Cycle Network or National Byway. These have usually been carefully vetted for traffic density and danger points, and in the case of the National Cycle Network may have been traffic-calmed or improved at intersections with busy roads. Alternatively, if you enjoy maps then why not plan a route for yourself? An Ordnance Survey Landranger Map (1:50,000 scale) is the best for this. It will not take you much time to learn how to identify which of the 'yellow' roads are best for cycling. One fairly serious shortcoming of Ordnance Survey maps is the situation with 'white' roads. These are roads or tracks where it is impossible to tell from the map whether the public has access or not. Thankfully, Ordnance Survey is now starting to improve this situation on its series of Explorer Maps (1:25,000 scale).

CYCLING OFF-ROAD ON PUBLIC RIGHTS OF WAY

You can of course cycle on bridleways (but you must give way to horse riders and pedestrians), Roads Used as Public Paths (RUPPs) and Byways Open to All Traffic (BOATs). Although traffic may be free to use the latter classifications, it is fairly rare to encounter a vehicle, but the surface can be expected to be very variable. The incidence of these rights of way that are usable by cyclists varies considerably according to the topography and different subsoils of each area.

DISMANTLED RAILWAYS

These are ideal for family cycling as they are usually flat, ideally surfaced and well drained. Some stretches of the Meon Valley Cycle Route and the Test Way, for example, are almost entirely intact, and virtually uninterrupted cycling can be enjoyed for many miles, but others have had their bridges removed which can make a dismantled railway ride frustratingly hard work. If you study an Ordnance Survey map you will see many dismantled railway routes that could have been made into cycle trails to form a ready-made national cycle network but many of them have now been built on, or their course has become extinguished beyond recovery. The loss of these routes, largely during the 'Beeching cuts', was such a short-sighted policy.

CANAL TOWPATHS

Canal towpaths are excellent for cycling as they provide a flat route, there is always something going on in a peaceful sort of way and there is an abundance of flora and fauna. Unfortunately, the surface of the towpaths can be changeable, often varying from tarmac to mud. There is only one cyclable canal in Hampshire and Dorset — the Basingstoke Canal — so opportunities are necessarily limited. This canal is operated by the Basingstoke Canal Authority and no cycling permit is required, although it is a permissive path as far as cyclists are concerned and permission to use it could be withdrawn.

FORESTRY COMMISSION

The Forestry Commission (FC) was established in 1919 to ensure an adequate supply of timber for the nation's needs. At the time it was considered

Below:
Downhill all the way at this point.

that the long period between planting and felling made this an unsuitable matter to entrust to the response of free enterprise to supply and demand. It is the largest landowner in the United Kingdom and owns holdings of over 800,000 hectares and advises private owners on the management of 400,000 hectares. Many areas of woodland owned or managed by the Forestry Commission have gravelled roads. These are well-engineered routes designed to enable timber removal by large lorries. Forestry Commission land therefore offers considerable scope for peaceful traffic-free enjoyment by the cyclist. When you are in forested areas you will see many references to 'Forest Enterprise'. This is an agency of the Forestry Commission.

Of course there are a great number of public rights of way on land owned or managed by the Forestry Commission and you have an inalienable right to cycle on bridleways, BOATs (Byways Open to All Traffic) and RUPPs (Roads Used as Public Paths) irrespective of who is the landowner. You must of course give way to horses and walkers on bridleways. Cycling on routes other than public rights of way can be done provided that the Forestry Commission has given permission — these routes are therefore known as 'permissive routes'. A permissive route exists only while the landowner gives permission for use, which in theory can be withdrawn at any time.

Generally, the enlightened view of the Forestry Commission is that cycling is consistent with the use of forests for quiet enjoyment and therefore its policy is to allow cycling unless public access is restricted by title conditions or forestry operations. The precise situation will vary in each piece of woodland depending on such things as whether the Commission owns the land or leases it, the existence of sporting rights, the size of the woodland block and the nature of the subsoil. The situation is therefore one of a delicate balance between forestry needs, conservation of wildlife, sporting needs, riding, walking and cycling.

The general rule is that you may cycle on public rights of way (except footpaths). You may also cycle on the forestry roads provided there is no sign restricting public access — for example for sporting reasons or forestry operations — or specifically restricting cycling on, for example, a walkers' trail. An increasing number of forest areas have waymarked trails for cyclists to use. Basically, if you use your common sense, and follow its cycle code, you will be welcomed by the Forestry Commission. Its cycle code is:

- Expect the unexpected. Keep your speed down.
- Remember other vehicles use forest roads as well as you!
- Give way to walkers — be friendly towards other forest users.
- Hail a horse and avoid an accident!
- Keep away from all forest operations.
- Do not pass any vehicles loading timber until you have been told to do so.
- Footpaths are for walkers only!
- Cycle with care and you can come back again!

When cycling or walking, it is fairly rare for me to become lost, but when I do it is always in woodland. There are usually no distinct landmarks by which you can navigate and it is less easy to sight the sun which also makes navigation difficult. So a little care is needed in the larger areas of woodland like the New Forest if you are not to run the risk of becoming totally disorientated. I would suggest that if you intend to explore a particular area of woodland and wish to plan a route using gravelled roads then you should either obtain a detailed leaflet from the Forestry Commission — if there is one available — or alternatively buy the 1:25,000 scale Explorer or Outdoor Leisure Map for the area.

The Forestry Commission produces a leaflet *Cycling in the Forest*. This is a national guide that shows the main off-road cycle locations on Forestry Commission land throughout Great Britain. It is available from local Forestry Commission offices or by phoning 01313 340303.

Forestry Commission land in Hampshire and Dorset falls under two administrative areas:

Southeast England Forest District

This area covers all of Hampshire with the exception of the New Forest. The main cycling opportunities falling in this area are:

- Alice Holt Woodland Park (FC1 on location map). This is situated on the Hampshire/Surrey border alongside the A325 just southwest of Farnham, and is an ancient forest that once supplied oak for building ships of the Royal Navy. There are good opportunities for cycling, with waymarked off-road trails and gravel tracks, and these are covered in the park leaflet. Bicycles can be hired from Pedalbikeaway at the Forest Centre (tel: 07775 840807).

- Queen Elizabeth Country Park (FC2 on location map). The park forms part of the South Downs and covers 576 hectares of beautiful downland and forested countryside. There are waymarked off-road cycling trails and Hampshire County Council has produced a leaflet as part of its Off-Road Cycle Trail Pack. There is also a visitor centre, gift shop and café, and cycle hire is available. Contact the visitor centre for more information (tel: 023 9259 5040).

- West Walk (FC3 on location map). West Walk, although now only a tiny fragment, is the largest remaining part of the former Royal Forest of Bere. This originally stretched from the River Test at King's Somborne in the west, to Rowlands Castle in the east and was 7 to 8 miles wide. West Walk has waymarked cycle trails and can be accessed from the A32 Meon Valley road, north of Wickham, or at Hundred Acres.

Above:
Rush hour in the New Forest?

the visitor centre. The park is 10 miles north of Bournemouth at Horton Road, Ashley Heath, Ringwood, Hants BH24 2ET (tel: 01425 470721 for information point and wardens' office).

The New Forest District
This area covers the New Forest and Dorset. The main cycling opportunities falling in this area are:

• The New Forest (FC4 on location map). There are extensive cycling opportunities in the New Forest, and a large number of cycle hire shops. One of the major factors that makes the forest so popular with cyclists is the 40mph speed limit on unfenced roads that has made it a safer place to cycle. There is also an extensive gravel track network of excellently waymarked routes. These either link villages or enable you to design your own routes through the forest. Also certain roads have been classified by Hampshire County Council as offering a degree of safe cycling. All of these routes are contained in the publication *Cycling in the New Forest — The Network Map* and this is available from the Forestry Commission, The Queen's House, Lyndhurst, Hampshire SO43 7NH (tel: 023 8028 3141). It is also widely available from local tourist information centres, cycle hire shops, camp sites and other outlets in the area. Please note that off-road cycling in the New Forest is permitted only on the waymarked routes.

• Moors Valley Country Park (FC5 on location map). Four virtually traffic-free, waymarked short cycle routes have been laid out, and by various permutations these provide opportunities for rides of from 2 to 6 miles. There is a cycle hire shop at the visitor centre. The park is 10 miles north of Bournemouth at Horton Road, Ashley Heath, Ringwood, Hants BH24 2ET (tel: 01425 470721 for information point and wardens' office).

SO WHAT MAKES A 'GREAT' CYCLE ROUTE?

Firstly, it is important to be safe on your ride and that means minimising the amount of traffic that you are likely to experience. At the start of the 21st century, traffic in Britain is greater than ever before and there seems to be little hope of this trend being reversed. The last thing that the cyclist wants is to share his or her day with traffic. My idea of cycling is to get away from traffic and the rides in this book are aimed at doing just that — either by using traffic-free routes or the quietest of country lanes. Secondly, if you have young children, then hills are an important factor — they are basically not a good idea. In Hampshire and Dorset it is not possible to design cycle routes with no hills at all, but it is possible to minimise them. One way of doing this is to follow old railway lines; another way is to utilise roads that follow river valleys or canals. We learnt this lesson on an organised cycling holiday a few years ago. Friends sniggered when we said that we were going cycling in Bavaria, but the operator had cleverly designed most of the routes to follow quiet roads that were situated in slowly descending river valleys. And the really clever part was at the halfway point of the 10-day holiday when we had lost most of our altitude. We put our bikes in the guard's van of the train and were simply carried to the top of another river valley, where we again spent the next few days in gentle descent. You will find that if there is a quiet road that follows a watercourse in Hampshire or Dorset that is suitable for cycling, then one of the routes of this book will follow it. The third factor in a 'great' cycle route for families is the surface. The idea of off-road cycling is attractive and it can be very rewarding, but is often too tough for young children or the inexperienced cyclist. For this reason, there are very few miles of cycling in this book that take place on unsurfaced bridleways or byways. The fourth and final factor is to have some sort of place of interest or refreshment as the destination of our ride. Wherever possible, I have tried to ensure that there is a picnic spot with a good viewpoint or a pleasant country pub around the halfway point of the ride.

LOCATION MAP

The 30 cycle routes in this book have been carefully chosen and checked to ensure the best cycling in Hampshire and Dorset. On pages 4-5 you will find a location map that provides a handy guide to where you can find the routes across the two counties. Also shown on the map are the main

Forestry Commission sites where cycling is encouraged.

CLOTHING AND EQUIPMENT

The Bicycle

Leaving aside the traditional sit-up-and-beg three-speed roadster, favoured by vicars and students in Oxford and Cambridge, but not really for serious consideration here, there are three basic types of bike available in the shops today that would be suitable for the potterer. Firstly, there is the touring bike, characterised by its drop handlebars and racks for carrying panniers. The mountain bike is rightly popular because of its ability to go anywhere, and it can now be bought with front and rear suspension, although this is not necessary for the rides in this book. Finally, there is the hybrid which looks like a mountain bike but has smaller-diameter wheels and thinner tyres so you get the advantage of the robustness of a mountain bike with greater speed. All of the rides on surfaced roads in this book could be undertaken on all types, but the ones with significant off-road content would make a mountain bike or hybrid desirable. If you are not certain of the cycle that you wish to buy, try hiring one first. Then when you have tried cycling and you find that it is enjoyable, go to a small shop that specialises in cycling and seek advice.

Helmet and Headgear

The potterer should wear a helmet if he or she is able to and should also try to ensure that children wear one. Having said that, even the modern lightweight ventilated ones are very uncomfortable and inconvenient on a hot day when sweat drips into your eyes. If you really cannot bring yourself to wear a helmet at certain times, comfort yourself with the thought that the health and fitness benefits of cycling are considerably greater than the actual chance of a serious head injury. As far as children are concerned the risk of a serious head injury is only about a third of the risk of a child experiencing a head injury from climbing or jumping. Nevertheless, a helmet offers a limited but significant amount of protection to the skull and brain if you fall off and hit your head on the ground. If you are not wearing a helmet in cold weather, you should always wear a hat as it will save a significant amount of heat loss.

Clothes

To wear, or not to wear, a pair of those infamous brightly coloured, body-hugging lycra cycling shorts for the first time is a big decision in the potterer's life. On the one hand they are a trifle over the top for pottering, and they show up all bulges, but they can be a real blessing. Cycle shorts wear well, do not have seams in the wrong places and are lined with chamois which sticks to your skin and prevents abrasion. Track suit trousers or jogging suits are a good alternative but they need to be fairly tight fitting. There are specialist cycling tracksuits which have zip legs and high backs but ordinary track suit bottoms should suffice. Jeans are not a particularly good idea. They have large seams in the wrong places, are too stiff and cold when wet.

One of the least practical items for day-long rides are cycle clips. If you like to wear ordinary trousers, and want to keep your self-respect by not tucking your trousers into your navy blue socks, then turn up the trouser leg a few inches. This looks acceptable especially with white socks or bare brown legs.

On the upper half of the body it is best to follow the well-established layer principle, taking with you several layers of clothing rather than a single thick item, and peeling off or on as required.

As far as weather is concerned, it is very advisable to listen to a weather forecast before you decide to go cycling and that way you can avoid the worst soaking. If you do cycle in the rain, no matter what you wear, you will find yourself getting clammy and probably wet anyway, due to the waterproof garment not 'breathing' fast enough to rid the garment of perspiration, despite the claims of many manufacturers. The old-fashioned cape can be very good as it allows plenty of circulation of air. If you take waterproofs, you will need to consider how you are going to carry them. A rucksack is feasible, but a better idea is a set of front or rear panniers, with the latter probably being the best. These avoid a sweaty back and have a low centre of gravity. If you think big and go for a large set of panniers, these could suffice for the whole family.

Footwear

There are sophisticated pedal and shoe systems which attach the shoe to the pedal. The shoe has a plate that locates into the pedal and will release from the pedal by twisting the foot sideways. But they are a bit specialist for the potterer and for the purposes of this book, trainers are likely to be the best bet.

What to Take

There is a minimal amount of kit that you need to take to stand you in good stead for most eventualities. The biggest worry is of course a puncture. To counter this you should ensure that you carry a pump with flexible connectors suitable for the range of tyre valves that you and your group may be using. I always carry both a puncture repair kit and a spare inner tube, on the grounds that if you are unable to repair a flat tyre your day out will be ruined. To accompany these, a set of three tyre levers are essential and an adjustable spanner with a capacity of up to about 25mm. In the heat of summer it is so important to remember to take sufficient drink to last you all day, so that you avoid becoming dehydrated. You should also consider the best way to carry this guide book, or your map. You could use a handlebar-mounted bag, which often has a clear pocket on top, or obtain a handlebar map carrier, which is rare but very practical. Alternatively, you could use a walker's map carrier, slung over your back. This sounds unlikely, but works quite well in practice. The minimal kit list that a wise family should consider taking should therefore include:

- Waterproofs
- A pump with appropriate connectors
- A puncture repair kit
- A spare inner tube
- A set of tyre levers
- An adjustable spanner
- A small screwdriver
- A spray can of cycle oil
- Spare jumpers
- Gloves (for winter, spring and autumn)
- A lock
- A rag or some 'wipes' to clean your hands after a repair
- Cycle bottles
- A map carrier or equivalent
- A small rucksack or pannier bag

Finally, the instructions given in the rides are recorded at specific distances. An inexpensive cycle computer would therefore be a useful aid.

CYCLE MAINTENANCE AND MENDING A PUNCTURE

This is not a book on bicycle maintenance but it is important to carry out certain checks before a ride. Checking for faults after a ride is even better as it will mean that you are much more likely to have the time to sort the problem out properly. This section concentrates on safety-critical checks which can be divided into three categories:

Brake Checks

Squeeze the brake lever and check that the brake blocks touch the rim after moving the lever between 1cm and 2cm from the rest position. If less, that is OK provided the rim does not rub against the block and make your cycling hard work. If the movement is greater than 2cm then the brakes need adjusting. Brake cables tend to deteriorate through neglect so these need to be inspected regularly. If the cable is frayed or seriously rusty it should be replaced immediately. Inspect brake blocks and ensure that there is plenty of material left, indicated by the depth of the water-dispersing grooves. Better quality blocks have indicator lines which show the maximum wear limit. One of the most common and annoying problems that occurs with cycle brake blocks is squealing. This is easily solved in most cases by repositioning the blocks so that they take up a slightly 'toe-in' position.

Tyre Checks

The rides in this book are not particularly demanding so the requirement is to have tyres which are properly inflated and have a full coverage of tread with no damaged sections. Mountain bike tyres will perform best if their pressure is varied according to anticipated use. Optimum grip for off-road use requires a lower pressure than minimum rolling resistance when on-road. Typical pressures for off- and on-road conditions are 40psi and 65psi respectively. If you do not possess a pressure gauge then squeeze the tyre sides. You should be able to press your thumb about 5mm into the side of the tyre. Inspect the tyre for adequacy of tread all around the circumference and for cuts in the sidewall and replace if there are any shortcomings.

Wheel Tightness Check

Many modern bikes now have their wheels secured by quick-release levers. These are extremely convenient and effective, but it is very important to ensure that they are correctly tightened, because failure to do so could be the cause of a very nasty accident. A correctly closed quick-release lever will curve in toward the wheel when tightened and the annotation 'closed' should be seen on the lever. In principle it is a cam device and provided it is tightened with enough force to leave a slight imprint on your hand, it will not come open on its own.

After a ride ensure your bike is thoroughly cleaned, checked and lubricated. Any problems should be rectified by a competent mechanic. Doing this after a ride should ensure that you take action in time for your next outing. Cycle shops usually require a few days to complete repairs and it is unfair to turn up and expect the mechanic to fix a problem there and then.

Mending a Puncture on a Ride

The first observation to make here is that this will be a very unlikely occurrence as you will be carrying a spare tube (I often carry two). It is surprising how soon you can become chilled and your willpower starts to go if you stop to repair a puncture on a cold day. You will need to have with you:

- A puncture outfit
- Tyre levers
- An adjustable spanner if you do not have quick-release levers
- A pump

NB: If you are merely changing the tube, follow Instructions 1, 2, 3, 10, 11 and 12.

1. Undo the wheel nuts. Release the brake cable if necessary, to enable the tyre to pass between the brake blocks.

2. Remove the tyre from the rim, using levers only if unavoidable — many mountain bike tyres can be removed without the use of levers and this is preferable to avoid the risk of pinching the tube and causing additional holes. If using levers insert

Left:
Running repairs.

them about 80mm apart and push them down together. Then insert the third lever and push it down. Remove the middle one and edge around the tyre until you can release the remaining amount of tyre by hand.

3. Remove the dust cap and valve securing nut and push the valve through the rim and then gently pull the tube out of the tyre.

4. Inflate the tube sufficiently to locate the puncture. Pass the tube close to your ear or lips to locate the escape of air. Mark the position of the puncture with a cross using the small crayon from the puncture repair outfit, or alternatively gently insert a small pin into the puncture.

5. Let the air out of the tyre and sandpaper the area vigorously to clean and roughen it. Select the minimum size patch necessary for the repair.

6. Spread a thin layer of glue over an area slightly larger than the proposed patch and allow to dry for 5 minutes.

7. While waiting for the glue to dry, check the tyre for the cause of the puncture and remove it. If you are unable to find a cause, check that the spokes are not protruding through the rim and rim tape. You should be able to use the distance of the puncture from the valve to guide you to the cause.

8. Remove the foil from the patch and apply to the tyre, pressing down firmly all over. Pinch the patch to split the backing paper and gently peel off — this minimises the chance of lifting the edge of the patch. Dust the area with some dusted chalk or talcum powder.

9. Inflate the tyre sufficiently for a test. Carefully check for further punctures — they often come in twos and threes — then deflate.

10. Place the tube inside the tyre and insert the valve through the hole in the rim. Inflate with a very low pressure to prevent 'pinching' of the tube. Ensure the tube is completely inside the tyre and then gently ease the tyre back inside the rim. Use the palms of your hands, if possible, to minimise the chance of a pinch, using the levers only if absolutely necessary. If using levers, double-check that there is no chance of pinching the tube between lever and rim.

11. Fully reinflate the tyre with a pressure appropriate to road or off-road use. Replace the valve securing nut and dust cap. Check that the cover is positioned correctly by spinning the wheel, and deflate and reposition if necessary.

12. Place the wheel into the frame of the bike and secure the nuts tightly. Check that the wheel is correctly positioned by spinning it and adjusting if necessary. Reconnect the brake cable and test the brakes.

TRANSPORTING CYCLES

Escaping from our towns and cities to go walking is easy. We gather up our boots and rucksack, climb in our car or on the bus and just go. Cycling requires a little more planning. Bikes need a rack for transport by car and you are not permitted to take them on the bus, so the whole idea needs more careful thought. We need to consider exactly how we are going to make our great escape from the pressures of city or town life to the tranquil pleasures of cycling in the country. The first means of escape is by the bike itself, but the chances of escaping from the town or city without dangerous exposure to heavy traffic are unlikely, unless you are fortunate enough to live close to the National Cycle Network.

Use of the Railway

Without doubt, the best way to travel to the start of a ride is by rail and 'let the train take the strain'. However, the position with regard to cycles on trains is complicated, seems to change often and depends on where in Hampshire or Dorset that you wish to travel. Most trains have a fairly restricted space for cycles and the number that can be carried varies significantly; booking may not be necessary, may be recommended, or may even be compulsory; and there may or may not be a charge. Broadly, there are five basic railway routes in Hampshire and Dorset and services to these stations are mainly operated by SouthWest Trains and Wales & West. Also a limited number of Connex trains operate to Brockenhurst Station, and Virgin Trains operates to Brockenhurst and Winchester. Each train operating company has a different policy and sometimes that policy varies within the company for a particular line due to the type of rolling stock that is operated. The list below is a snapshot of the situation in 2000. This may alter due to franchising or rolling stock changes.

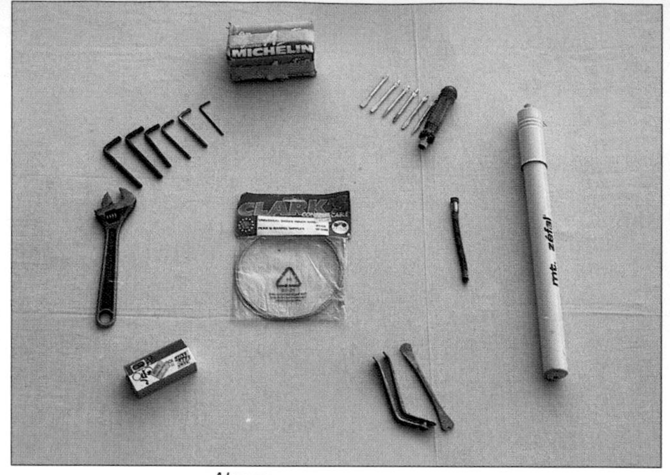

Above:
Cycle maintenance and mending a puncture.

- **Alton station — Waterloo to Alton line (SouthWest Trains)**
Bicycles and riders are welcome and there is no charge or need for advance booking. There could be some restriction on carriage of cycles in the London suburban area if departing from Waterloo between 16.30 and 18.30, or arriving between 07.45 and 09.45 on weekdays.

- **Andover station — Waterloo to Salisbury line (SouthWest Trains)**
Cycles carried only with advance reservation.

- **Brockenhurst station — Waterloo to Weymouth line (SouthWest Trains)**
Bicycles and riders are welcome and there is no charge or need for advance booking. There could be some restriction on carriage of cycles in the London suburban area if departing from Waterloo between 16.30 and 18.30, or arriving between 07.45 and 09.45 on weekdays.

- **Brockenhurst station — Connecting services operated by Connex**
A limited number of cycles is carried on all services except those timed to depart from London between 16.00 and 18.59 or to arrive between 07.00 and 09.59 on weekdays. No charge is made. Connex reserves the right to restrict the carriage of cycles on any train if the safety and comfort of customers is likely to be affected or if delays are likely to be caused.

- **Brockenhurst station — Connecting services operated by Virgin Trains**
Cycles are carried, but limited space is available and advance reservation (with a small fee) is required.

- **Dorchester South station — Waterloo to Weymouth line (SouthWest Trains)**
Bicycles and riders are welcome and there is no charge or need for advance booking. There could be some restriction on carriage of cycles in the London suburban area if departing from Waterloo between 16.30 and 18.30, or arriving between 07.45 and 09.45 on weekdays.

- **Dorchester West station — Westbury to Weymouth line (Wales & West)**
Cycles on this service are carried free of charge if space is available. Some restrictions at peak hours may apply. Wales & West provides a leaflet: *Cycling by Train, a Guide to Wales & West Services.*

- **Gillingham station — Salisbury to Exeter line (SouthWest Trains)**
Cycles carried only with advance reservation.

- **Maiden Newton station — Westbury to Weymouth line (Wales & West)**
Cycles on this service are carried free of charge if space is available. Some restrictions at peak hours may apply. Wales & West provides a leaflet: *Cycling by Train, a Guide to Wales & West Services.*

- **Rowlands Castle station — Waterloo to Portsmouth line (SouthWest Trains)**
Bicycles and riders are welcome and there is no charge or need for advance booking. There could be some restriction on carriage of cycles in the London suburban area if departing from Waterloo between 16.30 and 18.30, or arriving between 07.45 and 09.45 on weekdays.

- **Wareham station — Waterloo to Weymouth line (SouthWest Trains)**
Bicycles and riders are welcome and there is no charge or need for advance booking. There could be some restriction on carriage of cycles in the London suburban area if departing from Waterloo between 16.30 and 18.30, or arriving between 07.45 and 09.45 on weekdays.

- **Winchester station — Waterloo to Weymouth line (SouthWest Trains)**
Bicycles and riders are welcome and there is no charge or need for advance booking. There could be some restriction on carriage of cycles in the

London suburban area if departing from Waterloo between 16.30 and 18.30, or arriving between 07.45 and 09.45 on weekdays.

• Winchester station — Waterloo to Weymouth line (Virgin Trains)
Cycles are carried, but limited space is available and advance reservation (with a small fee) is required.

• Wool station — Waterloo to Weymouth line (SouthWest Trains)
Bicycles and riders are welcome and there is no charge or need for advance booking. There could be some restriction on carriage of cycles in the London suburban area if departing from Waterloo between 16.30 and 18.30, or arriving between 07.45 and 09.45 on weekdays.

• Yetminster station — Westbury to Weymouth line (Wales & West)
Cycles on this service are carried free of charge if space is available. Some restrictions at peak hours may apply. Wales & West provides a leaflet: *Cycling by Train, a Guide to Wales & West Services.*

The list addresses only services in Hampshire or Dorset that stop at the particular stations close to the ride. If you are using another connecting service at the start of your journey, then different conditions may apply, so whenever you take your cycles by rail, the best advice is to contact a railway information office as early as possible. Either contact the National Rail Enquiry Line for information (on 08457 484950) or one of the following numbers for advance reservations and ticket purchase:

• Central Trains	0870 0006060
• First Great Western	0845 7000125
• First North Western	08705 301530
• Valley Trains	No reservations
• Virgin Trains	08457 443367
• Wales & West	0870 9000773
• Connex	0870 6030405
• SouthWest Trains	0845 600650

If you do decide to use the train, make sure that you are on the platform in good time and report to the guard or conductor as soon as possible. It is best to wait three-quarters of the way towards the back end of the platform to spot the guard's van or bike storage section as it passes. With luck you will be seen and the doors will be opened. Prepare to load and unload your cycles yourself and be willing to move quickly. It is wise to tie a label on to your machine stating your name and destination. You should be most careful on Sundays as it is track maintenance day and it is important to ensure that the train will be running both ways without interruption. If a section of track is under maintenance, then buses are used to transport passengers and these are not permitted to carry cycles. Diversions are far more frequent during the winter months and during this time Sunday morning services can be quite sparse.

Transport by Car

If, like many of us, you are not lucky enough to be close to a railway station, you have only one way to get to the start of these rides, and that is to use a car. It is possible to take your bike inside the car, if you remove one or more wheels, but that probably limits the number of cycles to be taken to just one. There is really no alternative other than to consider a cycle rack. There are two basic ways of carrying a bike: a rear-mounted carrier, and by the use of the roof.

The rear-mounted carrier is probably the least expensive method, but you are generally limited to two bikes, sometimes three. The bikes mount sideways across the rear of the car, and the one big advantage is that you can see them during your journey. However, there is a tendency to make the car tail-heavy, and you must ensure that your rear number plate is not covered or you will be committing an offence. There are also regulations restricting how much your 'payload' can protrude over your rear lights. That is not to say that these carriers are not a good idea, as they provide a cost-effective solution, but it is important that you check and consider these things before you part with your hard-earned cash.

The other alternative is to carry the bikes on the roof. You can strap them down with bungee straps on top of a roof rack in which case they will quickly become scratched. The best but most expensive solution is to purchase roof bars and special cycle carriers that clamp to them. Without doubt, the best type of roof-bar-mounted cycle carrier is the type that secures the wheels in a channel that runs the length of the bike, and also clamps the diagonal member of the frame. These clamps are lockable and enable you to lock your bikes to the car. I have used one of these on a small car and have found the arrangement very satisfactory for carrying as many as four bikes. Most car manufacturers have roof bars and matching cycle carriers available as part of their accessory range. It is probable that buying equipment specifically matched to your car will generally provide the best, if not the cheapest, solution, although versions for multi-application are widely available from car accessory shops. Having firmly supported the advantages of roof bar carriers, there is also one disadvantage to be noted as I found to my cost in the lovely county town of Taunton, on an otherwise idyllic August day a few years ago. It is very easy to momentarily forget that there are cycles on the roof when entering car parks with height restriction bars, and this I duly did. Not only are many multi-storey car parks equipped with horizontal bars seemingly designed to cause maximum damage to cycles on the roof, but so, ironically, are many of the car parks specifically provided for many of the rides in this book. You will need to be vigilant if you use a roof bar carrier.

THE BASINGSTOKE CANAL

(A circular route starting and finishing on the canal)

The inhabitants of a little market town in Hants, where no considerable manufacture is carried on, have unaccountably conceived the idea that if a navigable canal was made 'some way or other' from there to London, they should emerge from their present obscurity . . .

From the *Gentlemen's Magazine* in 1778

Cycling as an amenity on the Basingstoke Canal towpath is not particularly well publicised. However, the towpath is open to cyclists as a permissive route and is a very enjoyable ride. The use of canal towpaths by cyclists is a delicate balance with other users, and cyclists are required to give way to pedestrians, keep their speed down and to dismount when riding under bridges that span the canal. The surface is made of quarry scalpings and is excellent all the way from Crookham to Greywell. This ride starts and ends on sections of the canal, and in between uses the network of country lanes and one short off-road section to complete the loop. I have two particular memories of the canal. One is of the huge herons that you see from time to time patiently fishing on the canal banks, often flying ahead of you in short hops. The other is of the surprising clarity of the water in the canal, especially at the Greywell end, contrasting with the cloudy water that you normally see in other canals. This is no doubt due to the fresh water flowing into the Greywell Tunnel from the chalk springs that provide a constant feed of water to the canal. The only less-than-perfect aspect of this ride is the irritating droning of Chinook helicopters from RAF Odiham. Rarely a moment passes without one of these large machines being somewhere in the sky above you.

BACKGROUND AND PLACES OF INTEREST

The Basingstoke Canal and the Greywell Tunnel

The Basingstoke Canal flows through the counties of Hampshire and Surrey. As originally designed, it ran from the Hampshire town of Basingstoke to its junction with the River Wey Navigation in Surrey, 37 miles away. The canal was authorised for construction in 1778 in the first years of the canal age. It was planned as an agricultural waterway and was to carry produce from Hampshire to London and to return from London with coal. In the long run the canal was a failure, but it had periods of prosperity. In the early 19th century, transport by barge was only half of the cost of wagon transport, but 10 years later costs had become similar and road transport was preferred because of its greater speed and more direct delivery to the customer. The canal has been extensively restored although there is a section at the western end of the tunnel that is not

Below:
Basingstoke Canal — Odiham Wharf.

Above:
Odiham Castle.

navigable. Of the original 37 miles, today 32 miles have been restored, from the Wey Navigation as far as North Warnborough in Hampshire. It is used as a public amenity catering for boaters, walkers, canoeists, anglers and naturalists. One of the most interesting features of the canal is the Greywell Tunnel. It is 1,230yd in length and was built between 1788 and 1792. The tunnel scheme was adopted in preference to an alternative, longer route around Greywell Hill. Without a towpath in the tunnel, bargemen had to 'leg it', while the horses that had pulled the barge all the way from London Docks were unhitched and led over the hills to the western entrance. The process of 'legging it' took up to 6 hours. The tunnel collapsed in 1932 and there were no attempts to revive it as commercial trade had ceased by the turn of the century. The tunnel is now home to a large colony of several types of bats. It is the largest known bat roost in Britain with over 12,000 bats and has the second largest population of Natterer's Bats in the world. Due to its darkness, constant temperature and lack of draughts, it is an ideal roost for the winter period. There are shafts in the tunnel, driven into the surrounding chalk, that allow the chalk springs to feed water back into the canal. For further information contact the Basingstoke Canal Centre, Mytchett Place Road, Mytchett, Surrey GU16 6DD (tel: 01252 370073). (Information based on *The History of the Basingstoke Canal* — Surrey and Hampshire Canal Society.)

Odiham Castle

Next to the canal, only a short distance into your ride, you will come across the impressive ruin known as Odiham Castle. Built in the 13th century during the reign of King John, it was here that the king set off for Runnymede to seal the Magna Carta in 1215. It consists of an octagonal tower, keep, moat and surrounding earthworks and is a protected site owned by English Heritage, but please note before you or your family explore, that there is a real danger of falling masonry.

Basing House

Again, close to the original route of the canal, but by a non-restored section, you will find Basing House. Although now a ruin, Basing House was once the country's largest private house, and belonged to William Paulet, Marquess of Winchester. It was the last of a series of castles on this site, which is evident from the remains of the foundations and cellars of the Tudor mansion and the earthwork banks of the castle built by the Normans, which still made a powerful fortress 500 years later. The Civil War brought ruin to Basing. There were lengthy sieges and massive bombardments before it fell to Oliver Cromwell himself. It is a pleasant, relaxing place to visit and has recently been enhanced by a re-created 17th century garden that brings life back to the ruins. Basing House is about 2 miles east of Basingstoke, close to Junction 6 of the M3. (Tel: 01256 467294 for further information.)

Starting Point: There are several possible parking and starting points along the canal. I started from Odiham Wharf Car Park (see below).

Parking and Toilets: Park in Odiham Wharf Car Park. This can be found in London Road, just off the High Street. This is free and run by the Basingstoke Canal Authority. It is not far from the centre of Odiham and is immediately alongside the canal. Other possible car parks along the canal are at Crookham Wharf and Winchfield Hurst (all without charge).

Distance: 20.3 miles.

Map: Ordnance Survey Landranger Sheet 186.

Hills: About one third of this ride is along the Basingstoke Canal and is therefore flat. The remainder of the ride has a few moderate hills.

Nature of Route: A significant part of this ride is off-road. The majority of the off-road portion is on the canal towpath and this makes very easy cycling as the towpath is well surfaced with quarry scalpings. The other off-road section of 1½ miles may have to be walked in parts, depending on the time of year. The surface is variable and can be wet after rain.

Safety: When passing under the canal bridges you are required to dismount, otherwise their curved nature and narrowing of the towpath could lead to a collision with a pedestrian, a nasty blow on the head or a thorough wetting if you were knocked into the canal. Also, some of the bridges are a little on the low side.

Refreshments: The Water Witch is close to the start and finish of the ride at Odiham. At North Warnborough there is the Swan — a free house. At Greywell there is the Fox and Goose and at South Warnborough there is the Poacher. In Crondall there is the Plume of Feathers and Hampshire Arms, and lastly at Winchfield Hurst there is the Barley Mow.

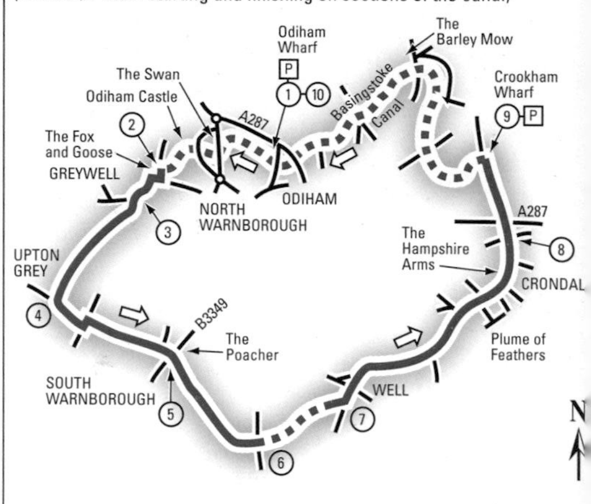

Nearest Tourist Information Centre: Willis Museum, Old Town Hall, Market Place, Basingstoke, Hampshire RG21 7QD (tel: 01256 817618). In addition, information about the canal in the form of a towpath trail leaflet, maps and circular rambles is available from the Basingstoke Canal Visitor Centre.

Cycle Hire: Action Bikes, 22 Winchester Street, Basingstoke (tel: 01256 465266). Basingstoke Cycle Works, Unit 1, Station Approach, Basingstoke Railway Station (tel: 01256 814138). Winklebury Cycles, Winklebury Centre, Basingstoke (tel: 01256 320645).

Route Instructions:

1. (0.0 miles): From the car park at Odiham Wharf locate the canal and cycle westwards on the old towpath (with the canal on your left-hand side).

2. (2.3 miles): Leave the canal and turn left over the entrance to Greywell Tunnel to follow the narrow enclosed path to the road. Join the road and at the junction, by the Fox and Goose, turn left into 'The Street' in the direction of 'Up Nately 1¼, Upton Grey 2½'.

3. (2.8 miles): At the Greywell signpost, turn left as directed to 'Upton Grey 2, Herriard 5'.

4. (4.8 miles): Turn left as directed to South Warnborough and Weston Patrick (the place names on the signpost are abbreviated) to cycle past the church and down into the village of Upton Grey. At the junction by the duck pond, turn left (no signpost at the time of writing) and after a further distance of approximately 100yd, turn right by the telephone box as signposted to South Warnborough (abbreviated).

5. (6.6 miles): In South Warnborough cross the B3349 by the war memorial, into Froyle Lane.

6. (8.5 miles): At the Sutton Common cross-roads, cross straight over on to an unsealed track indicated as 'Right of Way'.

7. (10.0 miles): You will meet a narrow surfaced lane with no signpost at the time of writing. Turn left here towards Well. At the cross-roads, by the disused well, cycle straight on as signposted to 'Crondall 3'.

8. (13.7 miles): After cycling through Crondall you will meet a give-way junction. Instead of turning left or right, go straight on along the small tarmac path that leads through to the A287. Taking great care, cross straight over into Crondall Road.

9. (14.8 miles): At Crookham Wharf, just before Crookham village, cross the canal bridge, and swing left to gain access to the towpath.

10. (20.3 miles): Arrive back at the Odiham Wharf Car Park.

THE SOUTH DOWNS WAY

(Along the edge of the downs to find some of the best pubs in the South Country)

Once the scenery and colouring of chalk country grip you, whatever your previous loves may have been, you are its slave for life.

D. H. Moutray Read writing on the charm of the downs in his *Highways and Byways in Hampshire*

Although the majority of this ride takes place in Sussex, it qualifies for this book because it starts in Buriton which lies just inside the Hampshire/Sussex border. This technicality is not the true reason for its inclusion, however. It is simply that, on a summer day, this downland ride is one of the most uplifting that could possibly be experienced. The route proceeds due east along the traffic-free ridge to Harting Hill, before descending to the fertile land below to meander back to Buriton along some of the quietest country lanes. During our meanderings, we pass (or preferably call at) some of the loveliest old pubs in the South Country: the Five Bells at Buriton decorated with its 'penny nails' around each stone; the nearby White Hart at South Harting for sheer atmosphere and comfortable 'oldness'; the Three Horseshoes at Elsted where you can sit in the garden and enjoy the most beautiful view of the downs; and the Elsted Inn at Lower Elsted where, if you are there in the mornings, you have the feeling that you are walking into somebody's house — such are the delightful smells of home cooking that emanate from the kitchen. You will notice as you pass through the villages at the foot of the downs that many of the older buildings are built of a very attractive white stone, often set off with corners of red brick. These villages of Harting and Buriton are often known as the 'Clunch Villages' — clunch being the name for this local creamy-white building stone that has such a beautiful appearance. It is interesting to speculate whether it is the nature of the stone or the fresh air of these parts that keep the walls looking so fresh and attractive.

BACKGROUND AND PLACES OF INTEREST

Queen Elizabeth Country Park

Centred around Butser Hill, which at 271m is the highest point in Hampshire, the country park covers 567 hectares of chalk down, scrub and woodland. There is a moderate 10-mile off-road cycle trail, and a 3-mile easy short-cut trail suitable for the family. There are also many walking trails and various country fairs and other events during the year. It has an excellent information centre with good interpretation of land use and a well-stocked shop and refreshment centre. Birds that can commonly be seen are kestrels, yellowhammers and whitethroats and it is one of the few areas where the golden pheasant is regularly seen. The park is situated 4 miles south of Petersfield on the A3 and is open daily from Easter to October and weekends from November to March (tel: 023 9259 5040 for more information).

Above:
Good views from the South Downs Way.

Uppark

This beautiful house of the most elegant proportions has been splendidly restored after the fire of 1989. It has particularly close associations with H. G. Wells whose mother spent two spells in service here, first as a lady's maid and then as a housekeeper. He spent a considerable amount of school holiday time here, and there are many stories about him in connection with the house. It was here at Uppark that H. G. Wells first revealed the direction that his career would take. During the period when the house was isolated for two weeks by a very heavy snowfall, the young writer produced a humorous daily newspaper called the *Uppark Alarmist*. He also entertained the maids and other staff in a miniature theatre that he made in the housekeeper's room. The romance and elegance of the house must have left a profound effect on the young Wells and influenced his progression toward the great author that he eventually became. The house is managed by the National Trust and is situated on the B2146 approximately 1½ miles south of South Harting. The house is open on Sundays to Thursdays from 28 March to 28 October (tel: 01730 825857 for more information).

Starting Point: This ride starts from Halls Hill Car Park — see below.

Parking and Toilets: Park in Halls Hill Car Park (free). If you approach from Buriton village, this is on the right-hand side of Kiln Lane where it intersects with the South Downs Way. (Kiln Lane is opposite the Master Robert pub in Buriton.)

Distance: 17.1 miles circular.

Map: Ordnance Survey Landranger Sheet 197.

Hills: The South Downs Way section of the ride has several short stiff climbs. There are less hills on the return section, even so there are a few that are testing. At the very end of the ride there is a very steep climb on Kiln Lane that returns you to the starting point.

Nature of Route: The first four miles of this ride follow the South Downs Way over a mixture of surfaced byways and unsurfaced bridleways where you will be very unfortunate if you meet any traffic at all. The remainder of the ride meanders around the quiet country lanes at the foot of the downs and in the vale that belongs to the River Rother.

Safety: Four miles of this ride is off-road and therefore it is especially important to wear a helmet when going downhill at speed.

Refreshments: The area abounds with good country pubs. Buriton has the Master Robert and the Five Bells. There are three pubs in South Harting, only a short diversion from the ride. In Elsted there is the Three Horseshoes and in Lower Elsted there is the Elsted Inn.

Nearest Tourist Information Centre: The County Library, 27 The Square, Petersfield, Hampshire GU32 3HH (tel: 01730 268829).

Cycle Hire: Owens Cycles, Lavant Street, Petersfield (tel: 01730 260446). Peter Hansford, 4 London Road, Horndean, Hants (tel: 023 9259 2270) and also at Winchester (tel: 01962 877555).

Route Instructions:

1. (0.0 miles): From Halls Hill Car Park, take the South Downs Way by following the route marked Dean Barn. After about 0.3 miles the surfacing ends and the South Downs Way becomes a track, until the Coulters Dean Nature Reserve, when it becomes surfaced again.

2. (1.8 miles): At Sunwood Farm, turn right off the road to continue to follow the South Downs Way.

3. (3.4 miles): When you meet the B2146, cross straight over it (taking great care as the visibility is bad) to take the track opposite and continue to follow the South Downs Way.

4. (3.9 miles): When you meet the B2141 (again taking great care due to poor visibility) turn left for about 30yd and then turn right off the B2141 to take the quiet lane down a steep hill.

5. (4.8 miles): At the end of the lane, turn right and continue through Elsted to pass the village hall and the Three Horseshoes.

6. (7.6 miles): At the Elsted Inn junction, turn left as signposted 'Trotton 2, Dunford 1'.

7. (8.5 miles): At a give-way junction, turn left as directed to 'Nyewood 2', along a road marked as a 'single track road with passing places'.

8. (10.2 miles): At a further give-way junction, underneath the power lines, turn left into Nyewood.

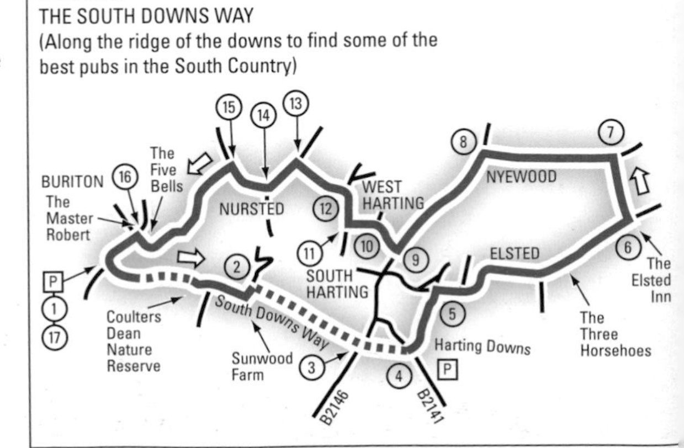

9. (11.8 miles): Avoid South Harting (unless you need some refreshments at one of the three pubs or the excellent village shop complete with delicatessen) by turning right toward West Harting.

10. (12.3 miles): By the old timber-framed cottage and ex-pub known as the Old Greyhound, turn left as directed to 'Petersfield 4'.

11. (12.6 miles): Turn right at the junction, signposted to Rogate.

12. (12.9 miles): At the next small junction turn left for Goose Green.

13. (13.6 miles): Bear left at the little triangular junction in Goose Green.

14. (14.2 miles): Bear right at the main road and re-enter Hampshire.

15. (14.8 miles): Turn left as signposted to 'Buriton 1½ miles'. This is a long and meandering route that will eventually lead you back past the duck pond and through the village.

16. (16.7 miles): When you are at the Master Robert junction, turn left on the route signposted to 'Chalton 4, Finchdean 6' to climb the steep hill and return to the car park.

17. (17.1 miles): Arrive back at the Halls Hill Car Park.

Below:
Four-legged friends.

Bottom:
The South Downs Way.

ROUTE 3

VILLAGES OF THE SOUTH DOWNS

(A circular ride from Rowlands Castle across the border into Sussex)

. . . I walked by devious ways to East Marden, between banks thick with the whitest and sweetest of sweet white violets.

E. V. Lucas writing about his impressions of the area in his *Highways and Byways in Sussex*

This ride is in the heart of the South Downs on the Hampshire/Sussex border. The route is mostly on quiet country lanes but about 4 miles is off-road on firm bridleways and byways. The ride passes through several South Downs villages with their characteristic brick and flint construction, and most of them have an excellent pub. For us, a high spot of this ride was the delightful village of East Marden. Although there is no pub here, you will find one of the quietest and most rural of hamlets consisting of a few homes centred around the old thatched-roofed village well, and where, I believe, there is not a single place where you can waste your money.

BACKGROUND AND PLACES OF INTEREST

Rowlands Castle

A lot of people wonder whether there ever was a castle in 'Rowlands' and, if so, what happened to it. The castle was a Norman motte and bailey type of which nothing now remains. Before the coming of the railways, there was still some stonework at a spot known as the 'Dell', a favourite picnic place for visitors who came to the village in their carriages, to walk in the countryside.

However, the building of the railway embankment to the south of the viaduct in the 1850s completely destroyed this site. The large Victorian residence known as 'Deerleap' that is situated next to Rowlands Castle Hardware covers up further remains, and this is where the castle was situated. Although it is not possible to visit it, behind 'Deerleap' there is a flagpole on a grassy mound that marks the spot as an ancient monument. The history of the village is made colourful by the story of the brutal murder of two customs men, who were met at the Castle Inn (a short distance from its present site) by the notorious Hawkhurst Gang and who were dragged through the countryside by horse, and beaten and whipped. One of them met his end in a shallow grave near Rake, while possibly still alive, and the other was thrown down a well at Lady Holt Park. As he was not dead either, the gang threw large stones and timbers down on him until they had finished him off. (Information based on *Rowlands Castle Past and Present* by Mary Jane Lomer, published by Lomer Enterprises.)

Kingley Vale Nature Reserve

This can either be reached from Stoughton or from the B2141, just north of where it joins the A286. There is a small visitor centre here which explains the significance of the reserve. It contains one of the most important collections of yew trees in Europe. Some of the trees are about 500 years old and measure 5m around their trunks. The reserve contains areas of chalk downland and also the more unusual chalk heathland. There are 200 species of flower here, including 12 types of orchid, as well as 57 species of breeding bird and 33 types of butterfly. There are also extensive earthworks and burial sites of Bronze Age kings from around 3,000 years ago.

Stansted Park

Stansted House and Park are situated near Rowlands Castle and our ride takes us past the front door. It is the family seat of the Earl and Countess of Bessborough and is set in delightful parkland. Visitors to the house can see the Blue Drawing Room, the dining room, the classically elegant hall and the restored kitchens. John Keats wrote arguably some of his finest verse in the chapel. The house is open on Easter Sunday and Monday, and on Sundays, Mondays and Tuesdays from May to September, 2pm to 6pm.

Starting Point: This ride starts from the village green at Rowlands Castle. There is a station in the village with regular trains from Portsmouth and London on all days of the week.

Above:
A lodge house at Stansted Park.

Opposite Left:
Rowlands Castle village green.

Parking and Toilets: Park around the spacious village green. There are alternative car parks (no facilities) near the second Stansted Park lodge house and at Stoughton Down.

Travel by Rail: It is perfectly feasible to travel to the start of this ride by train. Rowlands Castle is on the main Waterloo to Portsmouth line. For details of carriage of cycles on this line, please refer to the 'Transporting Cycles' section.

Distance: 18.1 miles circular route.

Map: Ordnance Survey Landranger Sheet 197.

Hills: This ride is in downland so hills are unavoidable. There are some steep climbs but most of these are short and sharp with no major escarpments.

Nature of Route: This ride takes place on very quiet country lanes that are nearly all unclassified. There are also two very pleasant off-road sections on bridleways and byways.

Safety: There are no special safety hazards on this route.

Refreshments: There are excellent pubs at 5.6 miles at Walderton (The Barley Mow) and at 6.7 miles at Stoughton (The Hare and Hounds). The George Inn at Finchdean is within a short distance of the end of the ride. There are three pubs in Rowlands Castle itself and also one of my favourite stops — the Coffee Pot — a cosy café serving excellent home-made cakes.

Nearest Tourist Information Centre: 1 Park Road South, Havant, Hampshire PO9 1HA (tel: 023 9248 0024).

Cycle Hire: Owens Cycles, Lavant Street, Petersfield (tel: 01730 260446). Peter Hansford, 4 London Road, Horndean, Hants (tel: 023 9259 2270) and also at Winchester (tel: 01962 877555).

Route Instructions:

1. (0.0 miles): Cycle from the village green at Rowlands Castle, with the Robin Hood pub on your left, towards the railway viaduct.

2. (0.1 miles): Take the right-hand viaduct arch, initially following directions to Stansted House — this is Woodberry Lane.

3. (1.8 miles): Having cycled through Southleigh Forest turn left at the junction at the end of Woodberry Lane.

4. (2.0 miles): Turn left off the main road as indicated to Stansted House.

5. (3.1 miles): At the second Stansted Park Lodge House, turn off right (marked 'private drive' but is a public bridleway).

6. (3.5 miles): By the wooden shed that marks

the entrance into the grounds of Stansted House, turn left to follow the line of the metal railings and thereby avoiding the metal gates.

7. (3.6 miles): Bear right off the tarmac drive to take the gravelled track with the pair of flint cottages on the left.

8. (4.2 miles): At the five-way junction carry straight on through wooden gates to continue along the track.

9. (5.3 miles): After descending the steep hill, turn right at the junction with the B2146.

10. (5.4 miles): Leave the B2146 by turning left on to the road to Stoughton and the Mardens.

11. (9.4 miles): Turn left by the village well on the road signposted to North Marden, Harting and Compton.

12. (10.0 miles): Turn left as directed to Compton and Up Marden, to wind your way up an incline that becomes increasingly steep.

13. (11.9 miles): Bear right at the junction as directed to 'Harting 3'.

14. (12.5 miles): Turn right at the junction with the B2146.

15. (12.6 miles): Turn left opposite Littlegreen School as directed to 'Finchdean 3' and climb the hill.

16. (12.7 miles): Turn off right on the road marked with a blue sign indicating 'Unsuitable for Motor Vehicles' then after passing the duck pond you pass a further sign reading 'Soft public road to Chalton'.

17. (14.6 miles): Where the gravelled track meets a junction, turn left as directed to 'Finchdean 2, Rowlands Castle 3'.

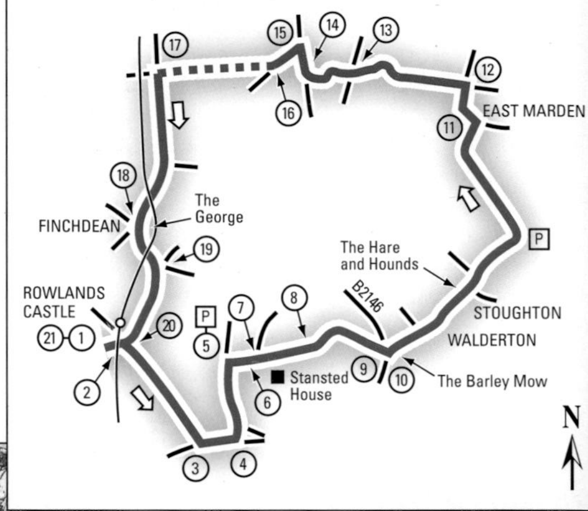

Above:
Descending a shady lane into Walderton.

18. (16.6 miles): Carry straight on through Finchdean village.

19. (17.0 miles): Turn right at the junction by Rose Cottage as directed to 'Rowlands Castle 1'.

20. (17.9 miles): Just after Castle Inn, pass under the right-hand arch of the viaduct.

21. (18.1 miles): Arrive back at the village green.

JANE AUSTEN COUNTRY

(A circular ride in the countryside around Chawton)

By the corner where the highways meet, with low lintelled door that opens on the road, stands a square unpretentious house, in part the village club, in part workmen's dwellings. A hundred years ago its roof sheltered the hand which limned portraits in prose of homely English life, reckoned among our classics.
D. H. Moutray Read describing Jane Austen's House at Chawton in his *Highways and Byways in Hampshire*

This is a short ride that has been restricted in length to allow time to stop and enjoy Chawton and Selborne. It takes place on quiet country lanes and between Oakhanger and Hartley Mauditt these are often sunken and can be pleasantly cool in the summer months. You may have a surprise and think that you are hallucinating when you are in the Oakhanger area and see the giant golf balls housing the RAF's earth satellite terminals.

BACKGROUND AND PLACES OF INTEREST

Jane Austen and Chawton

Much of the last eight years of Jane Austen's life was spend at Chawton and it was during this time that she wrote most of her published work, working on classic novels like *Emma, Mansfield Park* and *Persuasion.* She lived in this relatively humble red-brick house from 1809 to 1817. Until after World War 2 the house was divided into two dwellings, but it is now a private museum, administered by the Jane Austen Memorial Trust and kept very much the same as when Jane Austen lived there. It is a lovely house with six bedrooms. The visitors' entrance, at the side of the house, leads through the stone-floored porch into the drawing room and it is easy to imagine Jane, her mother and her sister Cassandra sitting there after dinner discussing the day's events. Two of the most interesting exhibits are two topaz crosses that were bought for Jane and Cassandra by her brother Charles with his prize money from the capture of a French ship during the Napoleonic wars. Outside, the garden has been restored to its original state. Jane Austen left Chawton a short time before she died and spent her last two months in Winchester, where her resting place is in the cathedral. Opening hours vary according to the time of year (tel: 01432 83262 for more information).

Gilbert White and Selborne

As you pass through Selborne, you will notice that it is delightfully set below Selborne Hanger (a hanger is a Hampshire name for a wood of beech trees growing on the side of a steep hill). The village is mainly famous for being the birthplace and home of the 18th century naturalist Gilbert White. *The Natural History of Selborne* is comprised of letters recording White's wildlife observations written to two other naturalists — Thomas Pennant and Daines Barrington. Selborne has changed little since White's day and the best way to climb the hanger above the village is to use the zig-zag path that was originally cut by White and his brother. At the top of the climb is a monolith called the Wishing Stone. The footpath and the hanger are both owned by the National Trust and are therefore open to the public. The Wakes house dates

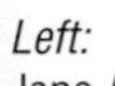

Left:
Jane Austen's house at Chawton - 'with low lintelled door that opens on the road'.

back to 1500 and is now a museum and memorial library devoted to the naturalist. It also features Captain Lawrence Oates who accompanied Scott to the South Pole and died with him, and Captain Oates's uncle (the explorer Frank Oates) who died on an expedition to Africa (tel: 01420 511275 for more information on The Wakes). If you are interested in art, there are galleries, a pottery and a craft centre in the village. St Mary's Church is open during the day. It contains two stained glass windows commemorating Gilbert White. The first illustrates St Francis of Assisi, Selborne and some of the birds described in *The Natural History of Selborne* and the second commemorates White's bicentennial anniversary. In the churchyard is the base of the famous 1,400-year-old yew tree which was sadly blown down in the severe storms of 1990 and also the grave of Gilbert White.

The Mid-Hants Watercress Line at Alton
This restored steam railway line runs from Alresford to Alton. The line originally closed on 4 February 1973, 10 years after it was scheduled for closure in the 1963 Beeching Report. The line recommenced working between Alresford and Ropley in 1977 and was later extended to run on to Alton. It was the watercress traffic from Alresford that gave the line its name. The town has, for the last 100 or so years, been the main source of watercress in southern England, and at its peak it is said that around 8 tons of watercress were sent every day to markets in the Midlands and the North. The line operates large locomotives due to the need to climb to Medstead & Four Marks station which at 650ft is the highest station in southern England. Steam trains link up with the national railway system at Alton (tel: 01962 733810; web:www.watercressline.co.uk).

ROUTE 4
JANE AUSTEN COUNTRY
(A circular ride in the countryside around Chawton)

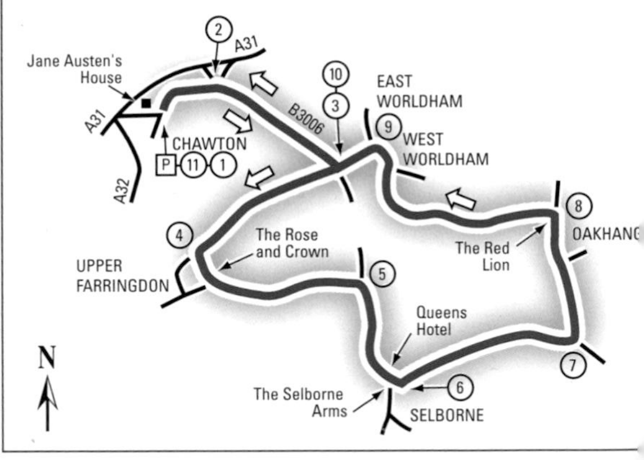

Starting Point: This ride starts from the visitors' public car park in Chawton.

Parking and Toilets: Park in the free public car park for visitors opposite Jane Austen's House. This is immediately adjacent to the car park belonging to the Greyfriar public house.

Distance: A short ride of only 14.8 miles.

Map: Ordnance Survey Landranger Sheet 186.

Hills: There are no long climbs but this ride is punctuated by frequent short hills.

Nature of Route: This ride takes place over unclassified country lanes with occasional short stretches on the B3006.

Safety: There are no particular safety hazards associated with this route.

Refreshments: Chawton has the Greyfriar pub and in Farringdon there is the Rose and Crown. In Selborne there is the Queens Hotel and the Selborne Arms pubs, and tea rooms at The Wakes (the Gilbert White Museum) and at Bush House. In Oakhanger there is the Red Lion.

Nearest Tourist Information Centre: 7 Cross and Pillory Lane, Alton, Hampshire GU34 1HL (tel: 01420 88448).

Cycle Hire: There seem to be no cycle hire outlets in Alton. The nearest that I can locate is Owen's Cycles, Lavant Street, Petersfield (tel: 01730 260446).

Route Instructions:

1. (0.0 miles): From the Chawton car park turn right to pass the Greyfriar on the right. After about 400yd, when you are alongside a pretty thatched cottage, follow the road as it swings right.

2. (0.6 miles): At the junction with the B3006, turn right.

3. (2.0 miles): Turn right, by what looks like an old turnpike cottage, as signposted to Farringdon.

4. (3.9 miles): In Upper Farringdon, turn left into Crows Lane and by the Rose and Crown,

turn left again.

5. (5.5 miles): Turn right as signposted to 'Selborne ½, Liss 5½' and enter Selborne village.

6. (6.7 miles): Having enjoyed Selborne, turn left as signposted 'Blackmoor 2½ miles'.

7. (8.6 miles): Turn left as directed to 'Oakhanger 1¼, Kingsley 3'.

8. (9.9 miles): Alongside the Red Lion pub, turn left toward West Worldham and Hartley Mauditt.

9. (12.3 miles): In West Worldham, at the junction by a triangular grass island, turn left as signposted to Alton.

10. (12.7 miles): Turn right as signposted to Alton to retrace your route back to Chawton.

11. (14.8 miles): Arrive back at the car park.

Right:
The base of the 1,400-year-old yew tree in Selborne churchyard.

Below:
Selborne church, burial place of Gilbert White.

ROUTE 5

THE MEON VALLEY CYCLE ROUTE

(A circular route from Southwick via the old railway line)

On rising ground between two branches of the Wallington River, is Southwick, a very picturesque village, with all the variety herring-bone brickwork, timber, plaster, tile and thatch can give the old cottages scattered round its streets without any set rule, sometimes square-fronting the roadway, or perched on a bank like a row of exaggerated beehives, one-storied, thatched, peeping through the roses and lilies in their gardens.
D. H. Moutray Read writing in 1908 on his impressions of Southwick in his *Highways and Byways in Hampshire*

This ride is as close to the perfect ride as you can get, and divides rather neatly into three sections. After leaving Southwick on some quiet lanes you join the gently sweeping B2177, where you can either use a generous strip at the side of the road or, in places, a parallel path to keep you away from the fast-moving traffic. On the next section you wend your way northward on the disused Meon Valley railway line where you will probably see more horses than people. The last third of the ride takes you due south, hopefully cycling with the sun in your face, on the quietest of country lanes that returns you to Southwick. There are several Southwicks in England, but I believe that this is the only one pronounced 'Suthick'. It is a pretty little village of old cottages, some thatched, that sits in the shadow of Portsdown Hill. The village benefits from the uniformity of its colour scheme — the Southwick Estate which seems to control the majority of the village, decrees that the doors shall be maroon and the window frames cream. In the summer months, Southwick is one of those villages where you will always find flowers and vegetables for sale at the roadside at prices that you would be foolish to resist. At the end of the ride when we return to Southwick from the north, the heavy clay land that we pass was once occupied by the Forest of Bere. The forest is now only a sad shadow of its former self. At one time it stretched from the River Test at King's Somborne in the west to Rowlands Castle in the east, but it has now retreated to three tiny patches.

BACKGROUND AND PLACES OF INTEREST

The Meon Valley Railway

I cannot claim to be a true railway enthusiast, but having lived through the final years of steam in the West Country close to the Great Western Railway, the experience has left me with a certain amount of nostalgia for old railways, so cycling an old railway line is always enjoyable for me. The Meon Valley railway line was opened in June 1903 and was operated by the London & South Western Railway. Although the permanent way was constructed wide enough to take two tracks, only one was ever built. In the early days the line was busy and carried more goods than passenger traffic, the main commodities being market garden produce — including strawberry trains in the season — coal, milk and livestock to the markets at Alton and Fareham. Trains became smaller and smaller, shrinking from 10 carriages to two in the 1920s. Competition from the commercial lorry also took its toll. The line limped on for 30 or so years, but closure began in 1955 although some isolated sections carried on until 1968. These days the route is an excellent facility for walkers and cyclists. Access is good and is usually provided by flights of steps.

Fort Nelson and the 19th Century Forts

Overlooking Southwick, although not fully visible from the village, are a number of massive forts that were constructed in a ring

Below:
A view of Wickham church from the railway bridge.

around Portsmouth to defend the harbour against a French attack from land. Five of these 19th century red-brick forts are strung out along Portsdown Hill (Fort Purbrook, Fort Widley, Fort Southwick, Fort Nelson and Fort Wallington) and they are generally named after the village that they overlook. Fort Southwick and Fort Wallington are still in use for various purposes, but the remaining three are now open to the public. At Fort Nelson is housed the Royal Armouries Museum. This records the history of artillery and includes the Iraqi 'supergun' and there are regular displays of artillery in action. The museum is open daily from April to October, and from November to March on Thursdays to Sundays only. (Tel: 01329 233734 for more information.) A little further east are Forts Purbrook and Widley. These have recently been renovated and are now multi-purpose activity centres. Guided tours are also available, but pre-booking is essential. Fort Purbrook is open daily all the year round (Saturdays and Sundays are mornings-only) and Fort Widley is open from May to September in the afternoons only. Contact Peter Ashley Activity Centres for more information (tel: 023 9232 1223).

Above:
A cyclist on the Meon Valley cycleway.

Starting Point: This ride starts from the Southwick village car park (free) that is situated behind the Golden Lion (see below for directions).

Parking and Toilets: Park in the D-Day Memorial Village Hall Car Park. This can be found at the south end of the village by taking the turning for HMS *Dryad* and then left before the retired sailors' cottages.

Distance: 15.6 miles.

Portsmouth Museums

The Portsmouth area is immensely rich in history and is imaginatively reflected in the city's museums where history comes alive. I never tire of going there when I get the chance. The City Museum and Records Office whose main display is 'The Story of Portsmouth' allows a glimpse of Stone Age Man, Saxon Man and the houses of various periods. The Overlord Embroidery in the D-Day Museum, inspired by the Bayeux Tapestry, is the largest work of its kind in the world and vividly recalls the 'longest day' when British, Canadian and American troops landed in their thousands on the Normandy beaches. Southsea Castle was constructed by Henry VIII in 1544 to protect Portsmouth against a French invasion. Its innovative design allowed the most efficient use of guns in defence, in a period when artillery seemed to dominate the scene of battle. The Natural History Museum is at Cumberland House and provides an illustration of the immense richness of nature around Portsmouth. Finally, the Charles Dickens Birthplace Museum has rooms furnished in the regency style of the period. There are three furnished rooms, a display on Dickens and Portsmouth and a small collection of memorabilia. (Tel: 023 9282 7261 for more information.)

Map: Ordnance Survey Landranger Sheet 196.

Hills: This is an easy ride with no significant hills.

Nature of Route: The first part is mainly on a fairly fast B road and a certain amount of care is required here. The second part is on an old railway line, and is therefore completely without traffic, and the final part returns you to Southwick, gently downhill on some delightfully quiet country lanes.

Safety: There are no significant safety hazards on this ride.

Refreshments: There are two good pubs in Southwick — the Red Lion and the Golden Lion. There are pubs, tea rooms and wine bars in Wickham (5 miles). For the Bold Forester (8 miles) you will need to leave the Meon Valley Cycle Route at ride distance 7.3 miles and cycle about 1/2 mile into Soberton Heath. Two other excellent pubs are the Horse and Jockey at Hipley (12 miles) and the Chairmakers Arms (13 miles).

Nearest Tourist Information Centre: The Hard, Portsmouth, Hampshire PO1 3QJ (tel: 023 9282 6722).

Cycle Hire: Owens Cycles, Lavant Street, Petersfield (tel: 01730 260446). Peter Hansford, 4 London Road, Horndean, Hants (tel: 023 9259 2270) and also at Winchester (tel: 01962 877555).

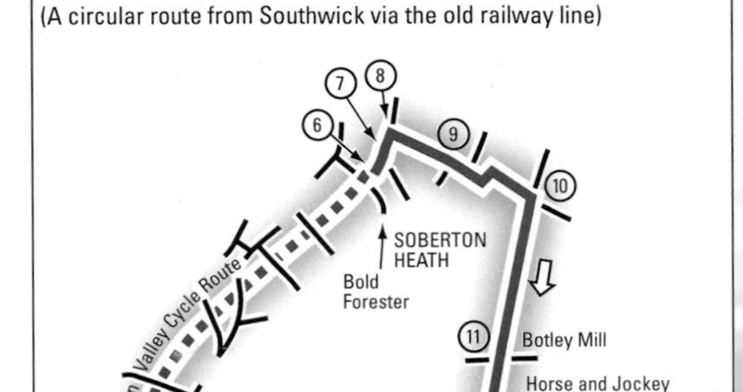

Route Instructions:

1. (0.0 miles): From the car park in Southwick pass through the wooden gate by the Memorial Hall to enter the village, turn right to cycle through the village with the post office on your left and then the road swings sharp left.

2. (0.5 miles): Just after you pass over the small Wallington River, turn right into Common Lane.

3. (1.7 miles): Where Common Lane ends, turn left.

4. (2.4 miles): At the junction with the B2177, turn right as directed to Wickham and North Boarhunt. Take care on this road on your approach to Wickham, as traffic can travel fairly fast. Fortunately, in many places you can take advantage of a parallel path or pavement which, although probably not a cycleway, would be safer if you have children in your group.

5. (4.9 miles): You will meet the A32 at a cross-roads, which you should cross to climb the steps at the side of the iron railway bridge. This takes you up to the Meon Valley Cycle Route which follows the line of the old Meon Valley railway line.

6. (8.1 miles): It is easy to miss your exit point from the old railway line as there is nothing particularly distinctive to record. Leave the line by a red brick-walled bridge with a lane underneath. The steps are at the far side of the left bridge wall. At the bottom of the steps, turn left and ride up to the cross-roads where you turn left as directed to 'Soberton 1¼ Hambledon 3'.

7. (8.5 miles): In Webbs Green at the war memorial, take the road marked 'Soberton 1 Droxford 2'.

8. (8.8 miles): Take the narrow lane on the right opposite a property called Millshares. This lane quickly rises above the road and, when by the telephone box, turns right and climbs steeply. You will be joined by a wider road from the left.

9. (9.3 miles): Turn left at the junction 'Hambledon 2 Denmead 3¾'.

10. (10.2 miles): Turn right at a small cross-roads as signposted to 'Southwick 4½ Fareham 7¼'.

11. (11.6 miles): At the staggered junction at Rudley Mill, bear left at the give-way junction and then immediately right as directed to 'Southwick 3 Fareham 5¾'.

12. (12.5 miles): At the T-Junction with a wider road (there will be a small river bridge on your left), turn left to pass the Horse and Jockey.

13. (13.0 miles): At the Chairmakers Arms, turn right into Forest Road as signposted to 'Denmead 1¾ Waterlooville 4¼ Catherington 5¼', and then immediately right again into the very narrow Apless Lane.

14. (14.3 miles): Where Beckford Lane ends, turn left and you will rejoin your original outward route.

15. (15.6 miles): Arrive back at the car park in Southwick.

THE BIRTHPLACE OF CRICKET

(The Bat and Ball and two of the high hills of Hampshire)

Assist all ye Muses, and join to rehearse
An old English sport, never praised yet in verse,
'Tis cricket I sing, of illustrious fame,
No nation e'er boasted so noble a game.
From the Hambledon Cricket Song

This ride is full of interest although a little hard work. We climb from the Meon Valley up to Broadhalfpenny Down to visit the ground where the great deeds of the Hambledon Cricket Club were done, to the nearby Bat and Ball where Richard Nyren catered for visitors at cricket matches and advertised his 'beef, ham, chicken and tarts for good appetites'. We also visit two of the highest hills in Hampshire. Old Winchester Hill (do not be confused as it is 15 miles from Winchester), an imposing hill fort standing 205m above sea level, and a little later, Beacon Hill at 201m. I am afraid that these pleasures come with a little pain, as they mean two significant climbs from river level to the high downs.

BACKGROUND AND PLACES OF INTEREST

Broadhalfpenny Down and the Bat and Ball

To people who have a love of the game of cricket, the word Hambledon will be well known. It is claimed to be the birthplace of cricket, although the nursery of cricket would probably be more accurate. The club was founded by a group of wealthy enthusiasts around 1750 and it had a brief period of cricketing glory until the end of the 18th century. During this time the club beat All-England, Kent and Surrey teams, and over a 10-year period beat England 29 times, the biggest margin being an innings and 168 runs. On one occasion the winning prize was as much as 1,000 guineas. The reason that the exploits of the Hambledon club are so notable is undoubtedly due to the Nyren family. Richard Nyren was taught to play cricket by his uncle, Richard Newland, (one of the truly great 18th century cricketers) in Slindon, Sussex. Richard Nyren later set up as landlord of the Hambledon public house known as the Hutt, later to become the present Bat and Ball. By 1771 Nyren had taken over a further public house in the village — the George — and he was well placed to provide the entertainment and refreshments for the matches. While Richard played a role of 'general' to the team, his son John was also one of the earliest of a long line of Hampshire cricket writers, and this ensured that the deeds of the Hambledon club were recorded for us to read. By 1782 the main action had moved to the Windmill Hill ground situated closer to the village, but the original ground and meeting place for the club continue to be the place that attracts the modern visitor.

Old Winchester Hill

It is worth dismounting your bike and taking the short walk to examine Old Winchester Hill, as the views from the ramparts are some of the best in Hampshire. This Iron Age hill fort — once known as Windover Hill — was built in the last 500 years BC, and encloses 5.7 hectares within the rampart walls. Before the building of the fort there was already a Bronze Age burial site here. The site has never been formally excavated but most of the barrows have been dug into. In addition to the views, the site contains a good mixture of chalk habitat, including open grassland and woodland, with juniper, yew and beech. There is also a wide selection of wild flowers, but conservation is the theme here, so please do not pick them.

Beacon Hill

There are many Beacon Hills in the south of England. Fires were lit on the top of these hills to warn the population, and no doubt the militia, of an invasion so that defensive preparations could be made. If you take a small detour to enjoy the perspective

Left:
Old Winchester Hill with Beacon Hill beyond.

from the hill, you will see that there is a line of sight to Portsdown Hill and the Isle of Wight and also commanding views of the Meon Valley. William Cobbett was most impressed by Beacon Hill, describing it as one of the loftiest hills of the country and it is probably best left to him to describe the view: 'Here you can see the Isle of Wight in detail, a fine sweep of the sea; also away into Sussex, and over the New Forest into Dorsetshire. Just below you, to the East, you look down upon the village of Exton; and you can see up this valley (which is called a Bourne too) as far as West-Meon, and down it as far as Soberton, Corhampton, Warnford, Meon Stoke and Droxford come within these points; so that here are six villages on this bourne within the space of about five miles.'

Starting Point: From the car park near Exton — see below.

Below:
The Bat & Ball, Hambledon.

Parking and Toilets: Park in the small informal car park by the Exton exit from the A32. This is northeast of Exton and lies close to the drive to Manor Farm. There are also car parks at Old Winchester Hill and Beacon Hill.

Distance: 17.5 miles.

Map: Ordnance Survey Landranger Sheet 185.

Hills: This ride starts alongside the River Meon and climbs almost to the top of two of the high hills of Hampshire. Consequently there are some significant climbs en route.

Nature of Route: The ride takes place mainly on the quietest of country lanes that it is possible to find in modern Hampshire, and on a couple of easy, short off-road sections. You will experience very little traffic and will find that you are on top of the world, often accompanied only by skylarks high overhead.

Safety: There are no significant hazards. Take care when crossing the busy A32 at Exton and Warnford.

Refreshments: The Meon Valley abounds with good pubs serving good food. The examples closest to the route are the Shoe at Exton at 0.2 miles, the Hurdles at Droxford at 2 miles, the Bat and Ball at 6 miles and the George and Falcon at Warnford at 12 miles.

Nearest Tourist Information Centre: The County Library, 27 The Square, Petersfield, Hampshire GU32 3HH (tel: 01730 268829).

Cycle Hire: Owens Cycles, Lavant Street, Petersfield (tel: 01730 260446). Peter Hansford, 4 London Road, Horndean, Hants (tel: 023 9259 2270) and also at Winchester (tel: 01962 877555).

Route Instructions:

1. (0.0 miles): Leave the car park near Exton and cycle along the lane parallel to the River Meon toward Exton village.

2. (0.2 miles): By Wyndham Cottage take a left turn, effectively continuing in a similar direction to cycle through the village, swinging left by the Shoe Inn until you meet the A32.

3. (0.5 miles): Carefully cross the A32 into Stocks Lane.

14. (0.5 miles): Turn right opposite a property known as Stocks Meadow.

5. (0.8 miles): At the end of Rectory Lane, by the post office letterbox, swing right and then immediately left to take the route signposted to 'Droxford 1½ Soberton 2½' and continue through Meonstoke.

6. (1.3 miles): At the top of the hill, where the road swings right, leave the road by turning left and passing through a barrier and turning right to join the old Meon Valley railway line.

7. (1.9 miles): By the rather ornate railway bridge, leave the line and descend to the road below — you should find yourself opposite the Hurdles pub — and then cycle up the hill and almost immediately take the unsignposted narrow lane to the left (marked to Watton Farm).

8. (3.5 miles): At the West End Down signpost, effectively keep going in the same direction (this is a large triangular junction). The road should be signposted to 'Chidden 1¾' but this is a Hampshire signpost and at the time of cycling the arms were swivelling in the wind, so just keep going in the same direction!

9. (5.1 miles): At the Chidden Farm junction, turn left as signposted 'Clanfield 2½', and at the next junction keep right (signposted 'Hambledon') and climb the hill.

10. (6.6 miles): At the junction with the Hambledon to Clanfield road, turn left and travel the short distance to the Bat and Ball pub and then turn left at the crossroads into Hyden Farm Lane to pass between the pub and the cricket ground.

11. (7.2 miles): Turn left on to a roughly surfaced lane — this turning is by a 'bends for 1 mile' sign. This lane provides very pleasant cycling, although you will notice a long and steady climb.

12. (8.6 miles): By the open barn, the road surfacing ends and at this point go straight on following the green lane for about 300yd until you meet the road where you turn left. This road takes you past Old Winchester Hill where good views are to be enjoyed a few yards from the road.

13. (11.1 miles): Turn left on the road that descends the hill into Warnford — this road is marked 'Single track road with passing places'.

14. (12.8 miles): At the junction at the bottom of the hill, you are greeted by the pleasant appearance of the George and Falcon. Turn left on to the A32 for a short distance. Take care as this is a busy road.

15. (13.0 miles): Turn right by the watercress beds and take the road marked 'Winchester 10 miles'.

16. (14.6 miles): Turn half left on to a narrow road that continues to climb towards Beacon Hill (the right turn at this cross-roads is marked to Riversdown House). Continue for about 300yd and at the next junction bear left. This road takes you past the Beacon Hill Car Park. A short walk of about ¼ mile from here will take you to the viewpoint of Beacon Hill.

17. (15.4 miles): Bear left up the hill to take the lane marked 'Unsuitable for wide vehicles' which takes you on a pleasant downhill ride into Exton.

18. (16.8 miles): Take the left turn marked 'Unsuitable for heavy goods vehicles' into the village.

19. (17.1 miles): You will find yourself back by the Shoe Inn where you will be able to retrace your route back to the starting point.

20. (17.5 miles): Arrive back at the starting point.

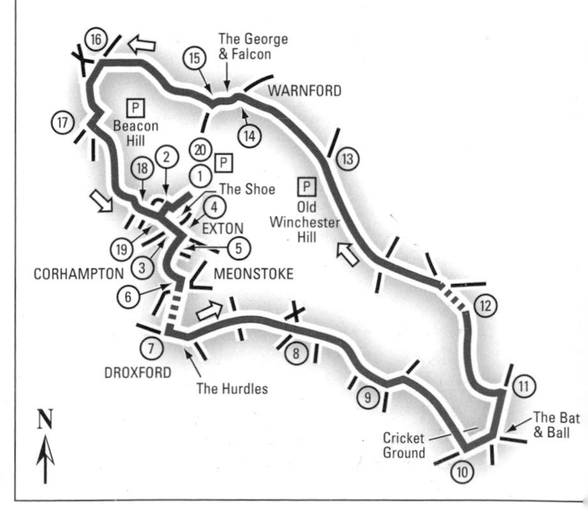

WINCHESTER AND THE RIVER ITCHEN

(A linear ride from Winchester following the River Itchen almost to its source)

You come a full mile from the roadside down through this farm to the Duke's mansion-house at Avington and to the little village of that name, both of them beautifully situated, amidst fine and lofty trees, fine meadows, and streams of clear water.

From William Cobbett's *Rural Rides*, published in 1830

This ride is a linear one from Winchester to the lovely old Flower Pots Inn at Cheriton. It is one of the best rides in this book as it follows the River Itchen for the whole length of the ride. When I first examined the Ordnance Survey map, with a ride along the Itchen in mind, the building of the M3 and the improvements to the A33/A34 on the east side of Winchester looked to have completely scuppered a safe ride, but examination on the ground reveals this is not so. Fortunately, there are pedestrian underpasses and pavements that allow you to negotiate your exit from the Winnall area of Winchester through to the lovely little back road that follows the Itchen from Easton to Cheriton, almost to its source, in complete safety, and is consequently made especially enjoyable by the lack of any significant hills. It visits some very watery places where there are often more ducks than humans, and there is a particularly beautiful spot near the Bush Inn at Ovington — see below. Directions are given only for the outward journey. To return you will need to remember your way and retrace your route to the starting point.

BACKGROUND AND PLACES OF INTEREST

Tichborne

The legend of the Tichborne Dole is locally well known and the charity still, I believe, carries on to this day. In the reign of Henry I, Sir Roger Tichborne's wife — a lady of wealth and great charity — begged her husband to set aside a sum of money to create a dole for all who asked for it each year on Lady Day. She was nearing the end of her life and was bedridden. Sir Roger was clearly not a charitable person and promised her as much land as she could crawl around, while a firebrand stayed alight. She managed 8 hectares and the field in the village is still known as 'The Crawls'. After such an achievement, she encouraged the continuity of the dole by placing a curse on the family if ever it was not distributed annually. Until 1894, 2,000 loaves were distributed annually, but, because of chaotic and unseemly scenes, money was handed out instead. An even more well-known story of the Tichbornes was a claim to the title made by a Wapping butcher. Another Sir Roger Tichborne went to South America in 1852. He embarked on a ship in 1854 to return to England but the ship went down with all on board. After a considerable time, and with leave to presume death granted, a new heir succeeded. Lady Tichborne, Sir Roger's mother, would not let the matter drop, and continually advertised for him in both English and colonial papers, also keeping a candle burning for him in his old room. She eventually heard from a man trading as a butcher in New South Wales, who purported to be Sir Roger. He was really Arthur Orton, a man of great daring and resourcefulness, who had learnt as much as possible about Sir Roger. The whole idea was quite improbable as Sir Roger, who was small with sloping shoulders, a narrow head and beaked nose, had miraculously changed into a 24-stone giant of a man. She met him in Paris, swore affidavits that he was her son and

Below:
Avington Park, near Cheriton.

promptly died. The case ran for 102 days and a verdict was given against the claimant. He was then tried for perjury and after a further 188-day trial he was sentenced to 14 years imprisonment, but not before the action had cost the family £80,000.

The Bush Inn at Ovington

They say you can't tell a book by its cover and in a similar way you can't tell a pub by its walls. Some of our best pubs can look a little tired from the outside and the Bush could be said to be one of these. I had only been there once before and from memory I do not believe that it is any worse now, it has just stayed the same. Inside, the general atmosphere is one of timelessness and comfort. There are large log fires in the winter, bric-a-brac and huge salmon in cases on the walls, and walls stained by the smoke of ages. The pub was built in the 17th century and is situated on the Pilgrims Way. Such is the unspoilt nature of the pub and the adjoining River Itchen that makers of films often come here for their location shooting. Perhaps the most famous visitors were Richard Burton and Sophia Loren who were here when the 1975 remake of the film *Brief Encounter* was filmed in the area. The naming of a pub as 'the Bush' is a very old tradition and it is perhaps the earliest of pub names. A bush outside a building was a sign used by the Romans to denote inn accommodation. In medieval times publicans also used it as a sign of an ale-house. A pole was horizontally mounted above the door and on top of it was a thick bush — this was also sometimes known as an ale-stake. This could be seen from a long way off and was a welcome sign for weary travellers. Even if you do not patronise the Bush on your ride, the river at Ovington is a very pleasant place to stop. Just wheel your cycle along the path to the river and enjoy a rest or picnic in the most beautiful of surroundings.

Cheriton and its Flower Pots

On the downs above Cheriton is the site of the Battle of Cheriton. This Civil War battle took place in March 1644 and represented a significant reversal for the Royalist forces. It was a very bloody battle and the lanes on the downs were said to have run with blood. The Flower Pots is the name of Cheriton's pub, and its unusual name is explained by its origins. It was built in 1840 by the retired head gardener of nearby Avington Park who is said to have built it with his 'golden handshake'. It is a bustling well-kept village local, surrounded by rolling Hampshire downland, where you are sure of a friendly welcome. The two little rooms have an atmosphere all of their own. Hops adorn the walls, the tables are of scrubbed pine and pews form much of the seating. For the last six years all of the ales sold here have been brewed in the micro-brewery across the car park and very good they are too. The traditional games of cribbage, shove-halfpenny and dominoes are played in the public bar. At one time the Flower Pots was not the only pub in Cheriton. The former HH Inn — which we pass on this ride — is now a private house but was once a place where 'rings' was played. This is a game similar to quoits but where rings are thrown at a board on the wall. The game enjoyed a revival in 1959 but ceased when the pub closed some time back. I have not heard of the game being played anywhere else in the locality in recent years.

Below:
The Bush Inn at Ovington.

Starting Point: This ride starts from the Durngate pay-and-display car park — see below.

Parking and Toilets: Park in the Durngate pay-and-display car park. This is on the northeast side of Winchester and lies off Wales Street. There is no charge for parking on Sundays and Bank Holidays. Winchester railway station is only 1 mile away from the start of this ride so it is possible to arrive by rail. It is also possible to park in Avington Park if you wish for a shorter ride.

Travel by Rail: It is perfectly feasible to travel to the start of this ride by train. Winchester is on the main Waterloo to Weymouth line. For details of carriage of cycles on this line, please refer to the 'Transporting Cycles' section of this book.

Distance: 9.8 miles one-way (19.6 miles there

and back). If you start at the alternative car park at Avington a ride of 6.4 miles (12.8 miles there and back) is obtained.

Map: Ordnance Survey Landranger Sheet 185.

Hills: There are virtually no hills on this ride.

Nature of Route: Apart from the initial section through the Winnall Industrial Estate, this ride follows very quiet country lanes through the villages of the Itchen Valley.

Safety: Provided you follow the directions carefully, you should be able to negotiate the A33/A34/M3 junction in complete safety using the footways.

Refreshments: In Easton at 2 miles there is the Cricketers Inn and the Chestnut Horse. In Ovington, at 6 miles, there is the Bush Inn. Tichborne has the Tichborne Arms (8 miles). At the end of the ride there is the Flower Pots Inn at Cheriton (10 miles).

Nearest Tourist Information Centre: Guildhall, The Broadway, Winchester, Hampshire SO23 9LJ (tel: 01962 840500).

Cycle Hire: Somborne Cycles, 3 Nutcher's Drove, King's Somborne, Hants SO20 6PA (tel: 01794 388327).

Route Instructions:

1. (0.0 miles): Leave the Durngate Car Park in Winchester — the Willow Tree Pub faces you — and turn left into Wales Street to cross the River Itchen via the Durngate Bridge, which will take you through the Winnall Industrial Estate.

2. (0.7 miles): At the end of the Winnall Industrial Estate, it is necessary to use the pedestrian underpasses and bridge to cross the M3 and A31. To do this you will need to dismount near the Shell garage (close to Homebase and Tesco superstores), cross the road to the opposite side and walk around the Tesco side of the small roundabout by following the pavement, carefully crossing exits from this roundabout as necessary. The pavement then becomes a footpath that passes under the road that forms Junction 9 with the M3. You cross the M3 via the bridge and then the footpath swings away from the road (under a TV surveillance camera) and passes under the M3 slip road. Emerge on the other side of the slip road and walk parallel with it for a short distance before the footpath turns right through a wooden barrier. You can then remount to cycle the very pleasant country lane which continues until you reach Easton.

3. (2.1 miles): At the staggered junction in Easton, by the Cricketers Inn, turn left and immediately right and take the road signposted to 'Avington 1½, Ovington 3½'.

4. (3.2 miles): Pass into Avington Park.

5. (3.4 miles): At the Avington junction turn left to ride through Avington.

6. (3.9 miles): As you leave Avington village, at the point where the road swings sharp left in the direction of the lodge house, bear off right to cycle with the golf course on your right.

7. (5.7 miles): At the give-way junction (no signpost) turn left to cycle down into Ovington and then after crossing the small bridge, turn right. (A left turn here would take you to the lovely old Bush Inn.)

8. (6.5 miles): At the junction with the B3047 turn left as marked 'Alresford 1½, — be careful as traffic is fast here — and just after the 40mph sign turn right on the road signposted to Tichborne. It will probably be best to dismount and use the islands to cross the road.

9. (8.9 miles): Pass through Tichborne, and at the junction by the bus stop turn right on the B3046 signposted to 'Cheriton 1'.

10. (9.6 miles): In Cheriton, just after passing the war memorial, turn right as directed to 'Winchester 7, Bishops Waltham 7'.

11. (9.8 miles): Arrive at the Flower Pots Inn and the Cheriton Brewhouse.

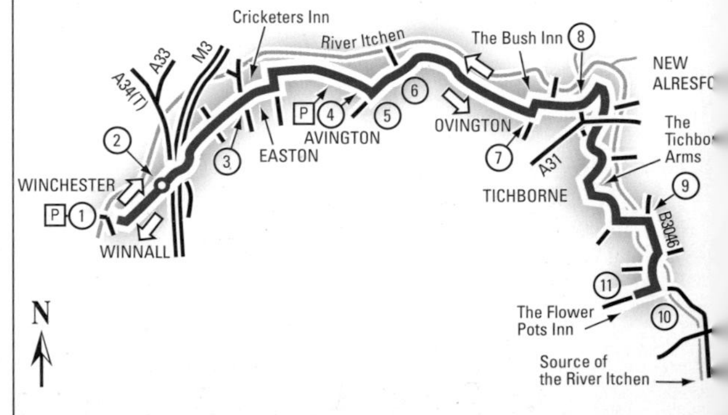

FARLEY MOUNT COUNTRY PARK

(A circular ride from the country park around the Winchester Downs)

Beware Chalk Pit, Beware Chalk Pit
As you go galloping over the downs Beware Chalk Pit.
Beware Chalk Pit, Beware Chalk Pit
The finest horse in Hampshire, Beware Chalk Pit.
The chorus from Graham Penny's folk song about the famous horse

This ride is on high and undulating chalk downland, and therefore has lots of ups and downs but without any really serious climbs.

You will also find yourself cycling along and then coming across the sudden straightening of the road, indicating that you are sharing the course of an old Roman road for a while. The ride commences along the southern edge of the country park and then touches the western edge of Winchester on B roads before meandering on unclassified country lanes through several pleasant villages, passing close to the Farley Mount folly then returning to the country park.

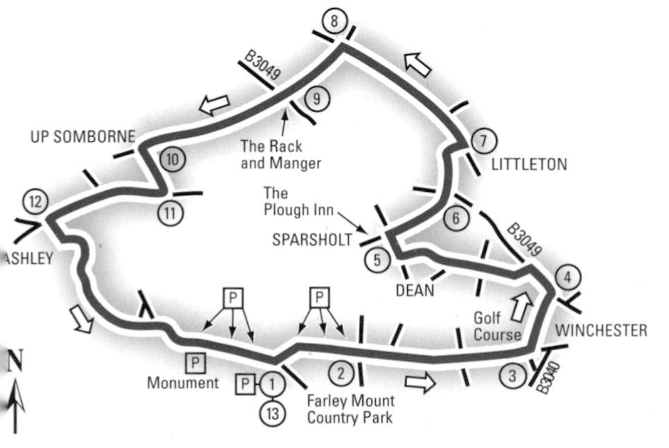

BACKGROUND AND PLACES OF INTEREST

Farley Mount Country Park

Farley Mount is a popular site for a picnic in the countryside. Set in beautiful rolling downland between the two chalk streams of the Itchen and the Test, it offers panoramic views of the south Hampshire plain from its 174m summit. At the highest point is a strange pyramid-shaped folly built on an ancient burial mound. This dates back two centuries and was erected as a memorial to a horse that survived a dramatic fall into a chalk pit with its rider. The original inscription, restored by the Hon Sir William Heathcote,

Below:
Lainston House near Sparsholt.

Baronet in September 1870, reads: 'Underneath lies a buried horse, the property of Paulet St John Esq. That in the month of September 1733 leaped into a chalk pit twenty-five feet deep a-foxhunting with his master on his back and in October 1734 he won the Hunters Plate on Worthy Downs and was rode by his owner and entered in the name of "Beware Chalk Pit".' The memorial, a pyramid with three blank porches and one open porch, where one can shelter while reading the inscription on a wet, windy day, was put up at a time when follies of all sorts abounded throughout the land. In the 1970s the memorial gained renewed fame when Southampton songwriter Graham Penny wrote a song about it entitled *Beware Chalk Pit*. The song was sung in the folk clubs of the south of England and had a chorus with a galloping rhythm (see quotation above).

Sparsholt

Sparsholt and the surrounding villages are set in a very rural part of Hampshire. Change has been slow and even now it is easy to forget the pressures of the 21st century in this quiet corner of southern England. It was only in 1897 that Sparsholt acquired its own water supply, when a brick and tile building with a storage tank and a mechanical pump was erected. Prior to that, in dry summers, even drinking water had to be carted up from Winchester. The only village supply was a 247ft well topped by a shed in which was a treadmill; it took two men 20 minutes to draw up the bucket! Sparsholt once had a waywarden — a man who kept the roads in good order. An inhabitant, Mrs Nellie Kirby, used to put a clean apron on every day and go gathering flints. She would put these in a pile by the side of the road for road mending. In 1926 the main building in Sparsholt, the Country Farm Institute, now the Hampshire College of Agriculture, was built. The college expanded during the 1970s when four halls of residence were added.

Winchester

The nearby ancient capital of Wessex and England lies steeped in history in the heart of the Hampshire countryside. First settled in the Iron Age and influenced by royalty since the 7th century, the city of Winchester has a wealth of remarkable architectural treasures. There are two surviving medieval gateways into the city. The magnificent cathedral was built in the 11th century and remodelled in the 14th century. It has the longest nave in Europe and is the burial place for ancient kings, such as King Alfred, and other notable persons, such as Jane Austen. The Great Hall is the only surviving remnant of Winchester Castle that was built by Henry III and later demolished by Cromwell. Winchester College, in College Street, was founded in 1382 by William of Wykeham, Bishop of Winchester, and is one of the oldest public schools in England. At the far end of this street is the Bishop's House, where the Bishop of Winchester resides. It is the surviving wing of a palace built in 1684 and overlooks the ruins of the 12th century Wolvesey Castle. The Hospital of St Cross is set beside the River Itchen. It was founded by Bishop Henry of Blois in 1136 and is the oldest charitable institution in the country. The 'Wayfarers Dole' of bread and ale may still be claimed from the Porters Lodge. Although these are some of the main historical sites in Winchester there are many other interesting places to visit. There are also cafés, restaurants, public houses of character and a thriving shopping centre.

Starting Point: This ride starts from the Junction Car Park in Farley Mount country park, see below.

Parking and Toilets: Park in the free car park known as the Junction Car Park in Farley Mount country park. There are several other free car parks in the country park that you could use: (in order) Spindle Trees, Westwood and Crab Wood. If you are visiting the Farley Mount monument, use the monument car park. After this there are Juniper, Hawthorns and Forest View car parks.

Travel by Rail: It is perfectly feasible to travel to this ride by train. Winchester station is on the Waterloo to Weymouth line and is only a mile away from the eastern corner of the ride so it is possible to arrive by rail and start from Instruction Point 4. For details of carriage of cycles on this line, please refer to the 'Transporting Cycles' section of this book.

Distance: 17.0 miles.

Map: Ordnance Survey Landranger Sheet 185.

Hills: This ride is in undulating chalk

downland, and therefore a number of moderate hills can be expected.

Nature of Route: This is a wholly on-road ride, and for the most part takes place on quiet country lanes, with a short distance on B roads around Winchester.

Safety: There are no particular hazards associated with this ride.

Refreshments: The Plough Inn at Sparsholt is only a few yards from the ride. The Rack and Manger is 10 miles along the route.

Nearest Tourist Information Centre: Guildhall, The Broadway, Winchester, Hampshire SO23 9LJ (tel: 01962 840500).

Cycle Hire: Somborne Cycles, 3 Nutcher's Drove, King's Somborne, Hants SO20 6PA (tel: 01794 388327).

Route Instructions:

1. (0.0 miles): Leave the Junction Car Park in Farley Mount and turn left to cycle along the southern edge of the country park.

2. (1.0 miles): At the cross-roads go straight on — the destination of this road is not identified except that it is part of the National Byway. The road becomes a single-track road with passing places as you approach Winchester, and you skirt the edge of Winchester Royal Golf Club.

3. (2.9 miles): Leave Sarum Road to turn left into Chilbolton Avenue.

4. (3.6 miles): Leave Chilbolton Avenue by turning left at the mini-roundabout to pass St Matthew's Church and then turn left into Dean Lane (signposted to Tegdown).

5. (5.7 miles): After passing through the pleasant settlement of Dean, at the end of Dean Lane turn right.

6. (6.4 miles): Cross straight over the B3049 to join a narrow and initially very straight country lane.

7. (7.2 miles): Emerge into Littleton opposite St Catherine's Church, turn left at this give-way junction.

8. (9.1 miles): Turn left by Crawley duckpond as signposted to 'Stockbridge 4¾, King's Somborne 5¼'.

9. (10.0 miles): At the crossroads by the Rack and Manger pub, proceed straight on (destination of road not identified).

10. (11.7 miles): Turn left as directed to Up Somborne. Climb up through the village and you will come to more open country.

11. (12.3 miles): At the give-way junction you will come to another broken signpost (par for the course in Hampshire). Turn right here to Ashley and King's Somborne.

12. (13.7 miles): Turn left as directed to Ashley and Farley Mount.

13. (17.0 miles): Arrive back at the Junction Car Park.

Left: Farley Mount country park.

WHERWELL AND THE RIVER TEST

(A short circular ride through the attractive villages of the Test Valley)

They are not long rivers — the Test and Itchen — but long enough for men with unfevered blood in their veins to find sweet and peaceful homes on their margins.
W. H. Hudson from his *Hampshire Days*, published in 1903

This ride starts from West Down Car Park, about a mile south west of Chilbolton. It is mainly an exploration of the Test Valley between Hurstbourne Priors and Wherwell. After passing through Chilbolton, it skirts the small army range at Barton Stacey, and crosses the A303 trunk road before taking a lovely little lane parallel with the River Test to Hurstborne Priors. The route returns on the other side of the river through Longparish. This is a place that lives up to its name. It was originally a nickname used in place of the real name — Middleton — which was the middle settlement of three with East Aston at one end and Forton at the other. After Longparish we come to the lovely village of Wherwell, before crossing the river and returning to Chilbolton.

BACKGROUND AND PLACES OF INTEREST

The Test Valley

Without doubt, the Test Valley has some of the loveliest villages in Hampshire. They are mostly small, with thatched cottages, each of different design and yet harmonising perfectly along the edge of the road, with small front gardens full of brightly coloured flowers in summer. Remarkably, they are largely unspoilt and much as they were in W. H. Hudson's day at the beginning of the 20th century. The river is, of course, world famous for its trout fishing and there are a few places that are open to the public for this purpose.

Wherwell

Wherwell, which is pronounced 'whirl' by most local folk, is perhaps one of the most photographed settlements in Hampshire. Its mainly black and white timber-framed cottages are crowned with fine examples of thatched roofs. The Old Malt House, Gavel Acre and Aldings are probably the best examples of this ancient craft. The Priory is a 19th century house built in the watermeadows on the site of the abbey, founded in 986 by Queen Elfrida who was mother of Ethelred the Unready. Elfrida may have decided to found a nunnery when she was filled with remorse after murdering her step-son so that Ethelred could take the throne. The nunnery prospered to the point when a settlement grew up around it. The abbey was destroyed during the time of the Dissolution of the Monasteries by 'the zeal or avarice of King Henry'. A few fragments of the original building still remain in the grounds of the house. Wherwell also has its own legends. First there is the story of the Wherwell Monster. It was said that anyone who saw the Monster — a mixture of toad, serpent and cockerel — perished. One would wonder how anyone could then have claimed to have seen it! According to the story, it eventually committed suicide after seeing itself in a mirror. Then there is the story of a fir in the Priory grounds that blew down in a gale. The roots when examined were found to enclose the skeleton of a man. Treasure supposed to be buried nearby was never

Left:
The start of the route at West Down Car Park.

uncovered; this was just as well because the legend had it that the discoverer could expect sudden death.

Andover Museum

The Andover Museum in Church Close is the perfect place to discover the long and interesting history of the town. The building itself is a fine example of Georgian architecture with a staircase that was much admired by Jane Austen. The museum traces the history of Andover from Saxon times to the present day supported by a wealth of fascinating archaeological finds. Exhibits include features on royalty, religion and superstition in medieval times, a 19th century period room and Victorian Andover including Weyhill Fair and a workhouse scandal. There is also a natural history gallery and an aquarium. Local artists exhibit during the year. Admission is free and there is a coffee shop. Next door, in the Victorian buildings of the old Grammar School, is the Museum of the Iron Age. This museum houses many artefacts from past excavations at nearby Danebury Hill Fort. The exhibitions give a vivid impression of what life was like for our prehistoric ancestors who farmed, fought, worshipped and died in Wessex. There is a small admission charge for this museum. (For more details of these museums, tel: 01264 366283.)

Starting Point: This ride starts from the Hampshire Recreation Car Park at West Down.

Parking and Toilets: Park in the West Down Car Park. This is 4 miles south of Andover, just off the A3057 on the Chilbolton road. The car park is approached by a pot-holed concrete drive. At the entrance to the car park there is a height restriction barrier, so beware if you carry your cycles on your car roof.

Right:
The River Test at Wherwell.

Below:
Shepherds Cottages, Wherwell.

Distance: 15.9 miles.

Map: Ordnance Survey Landranger Sheet 185.

Hills: This ride takes place mainly in the villages of the Test Valley and is one of the flatter rides in the series.

Nature of Route: This ride follows surfaced roads entirely and is divided almost equally between B classification roads and unclassified roads.

Safety: There are no particular safety hazards associated with this ride.

Refreshments: At the beginning and end of the ride there is the Abbots Mitre in Chilbolton. The Swan Inn at Barton Stacey is at 4 miles and the Hurstbourne in Hurstbourne Priors is at 9 miles. The Cricketers Inn and the Plough Inn at Longparish are at 10 and 11 miles respectively. In Wherwell, a short distance from the route, is the White Lion.

Nearest Tourist Information Centre: Town Mill House, Bridge Street, Andover, Hampshire SP10 1BL (tel: 01264 324320).

Cycle Hire: Behind the Bike Shed, 29 Charlton Road, Charlton, Andover, Hants (Tel: 01264 338794). Boltons, 8 Andover Road, Ludgershall, Wilts (tel: 01264 791818).

Route Instructions:

1. (0.0 miles): At the end of the West Down Car Park's concrete drive, turn right toward Chilbolton.

2. (0.9 miles): At the cross-roads at the far end of Chilbolton village, turn right into Winchester Street as directed to 'Newton Stacey 1, Barton Stacey 3' and at the top of the hill, turn left to continue to the Staceys.

3. (1.6 miles): Cross straight over the intersection with the B3420 and proceed in the direction 'Newton Stacey ½".

4. (2.3 miles): Just after Newton Stacey, you will negotiate a sharp left and then right turn as you cycle around the edge of the military range. Do not worry if the red flags are flying as this ride keeps you clear of the range.

5. (3.8 miles): At the junction by Barton Stacey Stores, turn left as directed to Longparish 2¼' miles. You will pass over the busy A303.

6. (5.7 miles): Turn right into Nuns Walk so that you can take the delightfully quiet back road on the east side of the River Test.

7. (7.7 miles): You will meet a wider road on its bend, turn left here for Hurstbourne Priors.

8. (8.2 miles): When you meet the B3400, turn left as directed 'Andover 5½' miles'. Take care here as traffic flows fast from the right.

9. (8.7 miles): Turn left by the Hurstbourne pub as directed to 'Longparish B3048'.

10. (11.9 miles): Take the right turn to the elevated road that enables you to cross the A303 safely (signposted Wherwell), and then right again having crossed it to join the B3048.

11. (13.9 miles): Turn sharp left (signposted B3420 Winchester 10 miles) by the attractive Shepherds Cottages.

12. (14.6 miles): Having crossed the River Test, turn right as signposted to Chilbolton and cycle through the village.

13. (15.9 miles): Arrive back at West Down Car Park.

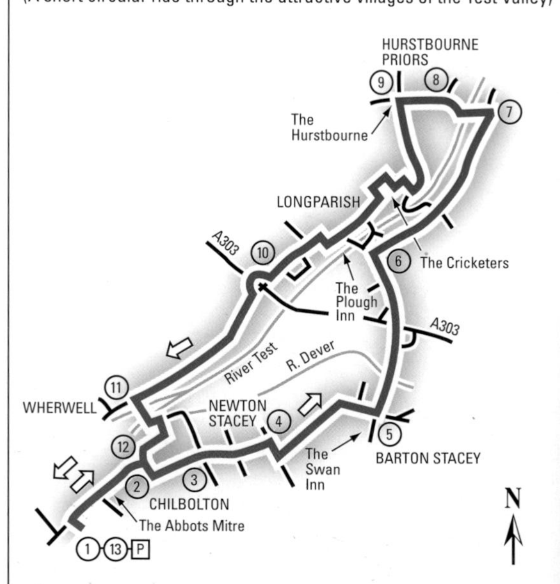

INKPEN HILL

(A circular ride using green lanes and country roads from Inkpen Hill)

Look ahead and the green ribbon trickles a little down the slope to enter the cirque of Walbury Camp whose rampart sweeps swallow-like the edge of the lateral headland thrown out to the south. This is one of the supreme moments of the downland traveller.
H. J. Massingham writing in his *English Downland* in 1936

Strictly speaking, I have cheated a little here as this ride starts just across the Hampshire/ Berkshire border inside Berkshire. OK, so I could have started the ride from one of the Hampshire villages on the route, say Linkenholt or Faccombe, but there are no obvious parking places there, and I always hesitate to park my car on the street in a strange village. Furthermore, the viewpoint from the west side of Walbury Camp is so good, and the parking is so easy that it makes an ideal starting point. So, I decided that there was no point in being put off by a mere chance geographical boundary. I am vaguely familiar with this northern part of Hampshire as my wife spent part of her early years at the Manor House in Linkenholt (which we pass on the ride), and so we have been back to visit the locality from time to time. The area really does have a lovely feel to it, quietly set in rolling downland, with beautiful deeply thatched cottages. One of the reasons that I was really looking forward to this ride was the chance of calling in at the Boot again, a wonderful old country pub of brick and flint, that my memory tells me was covered with a wonderful display of roses in the summer. Alas, I was to be disappointed as the Boot exists no more as a pub, only as a private house. I have since learnt that it has been closed for several years, so that left me a little deflated. At the time of writing, about 20 'Boots' a month are being closed, with many being sold off as private houses, so this is a worry. Having said this, it was still a very enjoyable ride, which I kept fairly short because of the initially difficult surface on the byway across the downs and the significant amount of hill climbing.

BACKGROUND AND PLACES OF INTEREST

Walbury Hill and Combe Gibbet

The starting point for this ride is at the Iron Age hill fort at Walbury Camp. The earthworks here are thought to date from about 750BC and enclose an area of about 33 hectares. Interestingly, the camp is the highest point of chalk downland in England at 974ft. These hill forts abound in southern England and were defended tribal centres. It is thought that a

Below:
View toward Combe from Linkenholt.

combination of wetter and colder weather, with a consequential reduction of available farmland and a rapid population growth, caused the need for these forts. Close by is the Combe Gibbet neolithic long barrow. On top of the barrow is the gibbet (an upright post with an arm used for hanging). The first record of the gibbet on this site was in 1676 when it was erected to hang a local couple — George Broomham and his mistress Dorothy Newman — who were convicted of murdering his wife and son. Since then, the gibbet has been replaced many times as it was such a prominent feature of the landscape and no doubt was seen as a symbol of law and order. About the same time as the deed that led to the gibbet being built, the surrounding lanes would often echo with the laughter of King Charles II's court party as he came to Combe Manor House with his mistress Nell Gwynne for weekends.

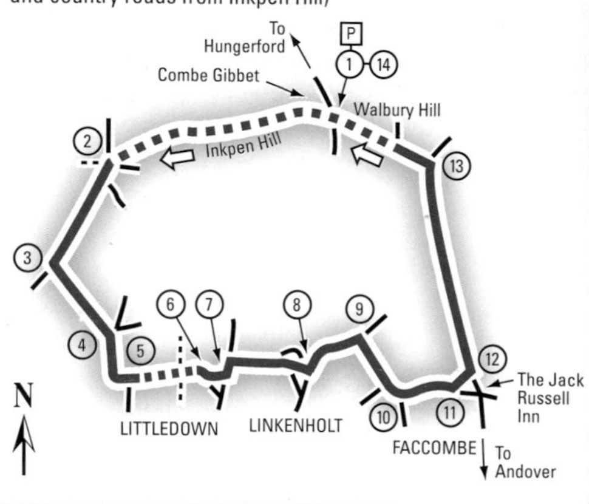

Andover

Andover lies in the heart of the beautiful Hampshire countryside but as it is one of those places that has been bypassed by the major trunk roads, the tendency is never to go there. This is a pity as it contains much of interest. Much of the old character of the town has been retained even though, over recent years, the town has grown considerably in size. The street market, which trades in the wide High Street every Thursday and Saturday, has a history that goes back over 1,000 years. The first recorded evidence of a market here is in the Great Charter issued by Elizabeth I in 1599. Although the old traditions of selling horses, cattle and sheep have been replaced with the selling of fresh fruit and vegetables, flowers, clothes and books, the market is still popular and an important feature of the town. The Guildhall, at the top end of the market, used to accommodate permanent market stalls known as 'The Shambles' and it is still used by various societies in the town such as the Women's Institute to hold coffee mornings, fairs and bazaars. As Andover was on the main coaching routes between London and the West Country and from Oxford to Winchester it is also well known for its coaching inns. In the late 18th century there were 16 inns and beer houses; today six of them are still trading. Many of the old coaching characteristics of these still remain so they are well worth a visit.

Sandham Memorial Chapel

Some 10 miles away from our ride, this chapel, built of red brick in the 1920s, is set amidst lawns and orchards with fine views across the Hampshire downs. The chapel was partly inspired by Giotto's Arena Chapel in Padua. It was built for Stanley Spencer — the artist — to fill with World War 1 murals inspired by his personal experiences at that time. There is no lighting in the chapel so it is best to visit on a bright day. Visits are by appointment only, on Saturdays and Sundays in March and November and daily except for Mondays and Tuesdays from April to October (tel: 01635 278394 for further information).

Starting Point: This ride starts from Walbury Hill Car Park (see below).

Parking and Toilets: Park in the car park at the west end of Walbury Hill. There are no toilet facilities on the ride.

Left: Walbury Hill.

Distance: 12.6 miles.

Map: Ordnance Survey Landranger Sheet 174.

Hills: This ride is situated in some of the best of north Hampshire and Berkshire downland. Unfortunately, downland rides always contain some hills and there is one significant one between Netherton and Faccombe.

Nature of Route: The initial part of the ride takes place on a byway running along the escarpment of the downs. This is initially easy cycling on a firm surface but after about a mile it becomes rutted and a little overgrown, so it may be necessary to walk for short distances. I say this as I fell off twice on this section, as I was unable to control the bike when the front wheel became determined to follow the deepest of ruts. Most of the ride, though, is on quiet lanes that are very pleasant to use. There are two other short off-road sections, and both of them, I would say, would provide a good surface in most weathers. The first is the approach to Littledown and this appears to be fairly well drained. The other off-road section is at the end of the ride, over Walbury Hill, and this is a very firm and cycleable surface.

Safety: Take care on the byway from Walbury Hill westwards. This has deep ruts and it is easy to fall off, as I did, when your front wheel becomes engaged in those ruts, or your pedals become stuck.

Refreshments: Unfortunately, there seem to be no tea rooms and, as bemoaned above, since the disappearance of the Boot at Littledown, there is only one pub en route. This is the Jack Russell Inn at Faccombe and is at about 9 miles.

Nearest Tourist Information Centre: The Wharf, Newbury, Berkshire RG14 5AS (tel: 01635 30267).

Cycle Hire: Hungerford Cycle Hire, 1 Priory Place, Hungerford, Berkshire RG17 0AB (tel: 01488 682206).

Route Instructions:

1. (0.0 miles): From the Walbury Hill Car Park (on the west side of the hill), head due west taking the byway that climbs steadily towards Combe Gibbet. This byway starts off promisingly, but soon begins to suffer deep ruts.

2. (2.5 miles): The byway eventually joins a surfaced road and then meets a T-junction. Turn left as signposted 'Fosbury 2 miles', and then cycle straight on at the next signpost which indicates 'Fosbury 1½ miles'.

3. (3.7 miles): After a gradual descent for a mile or so, turn left as signposted to Henley.

4. (4.7 miles): Turn right as directed to Vernham Dean 1¼ miles and Andover 9¼ miles.

5. (5.1 miles): The road swings sharp left and immediately right. At the point where it swings right, leave the road by taking the green lane to the left which passes under the high-voltage power lines.

6. (5.9 miles): Just after the green lane becomes surfaced you enter Littledown. Take the leftmost route as you enter this settlement to climb the hill.

7. (6.2 miles): At the junction by the house that used to be the Boot pub, swing left and then immediately right to 'Linkenholt 1 mile'.

8. (7.2 miles): Pass through Linkenholt with its impressive manor house, old school house and church. At the triangular grassed junction at the end of the village, turn left as signposted to 'Faccombe 2¼', Combe 2'; you will enjoy excellent views as you descend from Linkenholt.

9. (7.9 miles): After the descent, turn right as signposted to `Netherton 1, Andover 8'.

10. (8.6 miles): At Netherton Farmhouse, turn left for Faccombe (the signpost was missing at the time of riding the route), and brace yourself for a steep climb up to Faccombe.

11. (9.3 miles): Take the left turn that leaves the road at a slight angle as you enter Faccombe. (If, however, you wish to visit the Jack Russell Inn, avoid this turn and keep straight on.) Fork left again to pass on the left side of the churchyard.

12. (9.5 miles): At the T-junction after the churchyard, turn left to begin the steady climb back to Walbury Hill.

13. (11.9 miles): Leave the road by the small car parking area at the eastern end of Walbury Hill to take the byway over the hill back to your starting point.

14. (12.6 miles): Arrive back at your starting point.

ROUTE 11

THE TEST WAY

(Cycling the Test Valley on the old railway line and some quiet country lanes)

There are no more refreshing places in Hampshire, one might almost say in England, than the green level valleys of the Test and Itchen that wind, alternately widening and narrowing, through the downland country to Southampton Water.
W. H. Hudson from his *Hampshire Days*, published in 1903

The Test Way is a long-distance footpath that predominantly follows the River Test and runs from Totton, continuing as far as Inkpen Beacon just across the north border of Hampshire, in Berkshire. Like many chalk streams there are few rights of way along the valley for walkers or cyclists, as the river banks tend to be privately owned and remain the preserve of the rich. It is only recently that this beautiful stretch of the Test has been opened up to the public. The section from Stonymarsh to Stockbridge follows the old Test Valley railway line which was built in 1865 and replaced the old canal that ran from Redbridge and Andover. This railway was affectionately known as the Sprat and Winkle line and like many other old railway lines it was closed in the Beeching era

Right:
Cycling on the Test Way.

Below:
The Drovers House at Stockbridge.

Left:
The old station at Horsebridge.

in 1964. This ride is by far the easiest of a series of off-road trails that are promoted by Hampshire County Council and published in a series of excellent waterproof leaflets (further information in the 'Publications Available on Cycling in Hampshire and Dorset' section).

BACKGROUND AND PLACES OF INTEREST

The River Test

One of Hampshire's twin rivers which, together with its sister the River Itchen, drains some of the county's most beautiful countryside and never touches the alien ground of another county. The waters are clear and fast flowing, and it is one of the most popular game rivers in the country. There is undoubtedly something special about Hampshire's chalk streams as one sits on the bank watching the clear water glide over the beds of waving water weed, hearing the whirr of a fly fisherman's reel and, beyond the willows, the splash of a large trout or some other watery creature.

Mottisfont Abbey

This is now a house that belongs to the National Trust but was originally converted from a medieval monastery. An observation of the relative morality of Mottisfont and Stockbridge was made by a Cistercian monk who maintained that he could see devils. He found only one in Stockbridge Fair but found dozens in the priory at Mottisfont. When he caught one and asked about this he was told that souls were easy to come by at Stockbridge, but concentrated effort was required at Mottisfont to provoke even the smallest sin. So expect a perfect place when you visit. From mid-March to October, the abbey and gardens are open in the afternoons from Saturday to Wednesdays. In the middle of June, they are open daily (tel: 01794 340757 for more information).

Stockbridge

I prefer country towns to have a high street of good proportions and Stockbridge is certainly one of these. The street runs from side to side of the narrow valley. Some of the houses in the little town date back to Tudor times and you can find almost every style along the street — timber-framed, brick and plaster — and there are no two alike in size or colour. The valley here has provided a river crossing since earliest times, and a posting station existed in the Roman occupation. The bridges came later and the latest one was built in 1962. The name of the town does not come from a crossing place for cattle but means 'log bridge'. Nevertheless, large herds of cattle did cross here at one time and the biggest came from Wales, as they were driven to the great fairs of Surrey and Kent. The coming of the railways put an end to these large cattle drives, but to this day a notice can be seen painted on a former inn at Stockbridge advertising 'Gwair Tymherus, Porfa Flasus, Cwrw Da, a Cwal Cysurus' which means 'Worthwhile Grass, Pleasant Pasture, Good Beer and Comfortable Shelter'. The town was at one time famed for being a 'rotten borough' where the 70 voters on the electoral roll returned two members of parliament. A vote could be bought for about 5 guineas but inflation caused the rate to go up to 70 guineas in 1790. Richard Steele of *The Spectator*, when he sought re-election, was not successful because he reputedly never fulfilled a promise to present an apple stuffed with guineas to the couple who could first produce a child nine months after his election.

Starting Point: This ride starts from Stonymarsh Car Park (see below).

Parking and Toilets: I parked in Stonymarsh Car Park (4 miles north of Romsey on the A3057) which enables you to stop at Stockbridge as a halfway point. Be careful if you carry your cycles on the roof of your car as you could end up with a fine mess — I have known a height restriction bar to be sometimes fitted at the entrance to the car park. An alternative is to park in Stockbridge itself on the wide main street. The only public toilets on the ride are in Stockbridge.

Distance: 12.9 miles.

Map: Ordnance Survey Landranger Sheet 185.

Hills: There are no significant hills on this ride.

Nature of Route: The ride divides readily into two distinct sections. The first takes you due north on the course of the disused Test Valley railway line as far as Stockbridge and is completely flat. After a visit to Stockbridge you return via Houghton and Mottisfont using some very quiet undulating lanes that partly follow the National Byway.

Safety: There are no particular safety hazards.

Refreshments: The first opportunity for refreshment is the John of Gaunt at Horsebridge. At the halfway point in Stockbridge, there is a very good selection of places to eat to suit all pockets. These include the Vine Inn, the Langtry Tea Rooms, the Three Cups Inn, the Greyhound and the Grosvenor Hotel. At 8 miles in Houghton there is the Boot Inn, and at 11 miles in Mottisfont there are some tea rooms.

Nearest Tourist Information Centre:
1 Latimer Street, Romsey, Hampshire, SO51 8DF (tel: 01794 512987).

Cycle Hire: Somborne Cycles, 3 Nutcher's Drove, King's Somborne, near Stockbridge, Hants SO20 6PA (tel: 01794 388327).

Route Instructions:

1. (0.0 miles): From Stonymarsh Car Park, head north with the main A3057 road parallel on your right, proceeding through the dark green barrier. Continue over a variety of surfaces — all of them good — until you come to Horsebridge.

2. (2.4 miles): At Horsebridge the Test Way meets a road. Cross over to continue on the Test Way.

3. (5.4 miles): The cycleway ends to join a quiet road (Trafalgar Way). Continue to the roundabout where you should turn left to cycle through the centre of Stockbridge.

4. (6.0 miles): Leave Stockbridge by turning left and following the route signposted to Houghton. (This road is part of the National Byway.) You will pass the Drovers House, interestingly inscribed in Welsh.

5. (8.5 miles): Turn right at the give-way junction in the direction of 'Dunbridge 4¼, Broughton 2½, Nether Wallop 5¼' to continue on the National Byway.

6. (9.1 miles): At this point you should proceed straight on as directed to Pittleworth and Mottisfont and leave the National Byway that turns right at this point.

7. (12.6 miles): You will arrive at the main A3057 Romsey to Stockbridge road. Turn left here, to return to the car park. Be careful as this is a fast road.

8. (12.9 miles): Arrive back at the car park.

Below:
Cycling on the Test Way.

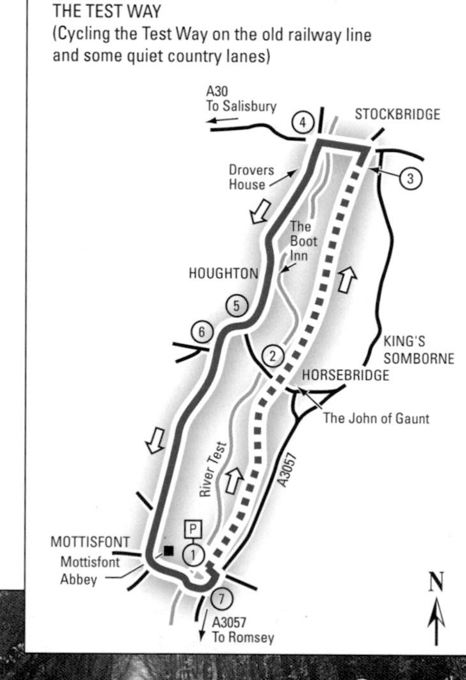

A RIDE OF FOUR RIVERS

(A circular ride near Andover visiting the rivers Test and Anton, and the Pillhill and Wallop streams)

At Upper Clatford, where a bridge leads over the clear stream, that gurgles a low song above the rippled weeds on its chalk-gravel bed, near a big willow and shallow weir, a shapely, branching yew and the little church stand in the quiet water-meadows with a venerable air . . .

D. H. Moutray Read writing about the village of Upper Clatford in his *Highways and Byways in Hampshire*

Above:
The River Anton near Fullerton.

This ride starts from Danebury Hill — a small Iron Age earthwork about six miles southwest of Andover — and explores the undulating chalk downland virtually enclosed by the Pillhill, Anton, Wallop and Test rivers. The pleasant lanes are often straight, suggesting Roman origins, but with little traffic to bother you. It is a ride of picturesque villages, with brick and timber cottages of deep thatch, often standing with their feet in water next to a stream. The Wallops, spaced along three miles of the Wallop Brook, are especially beautiful and were used as the setting for the Miss Marple television series. Longstock is also attractive with its deeply thatched cottages and distant glimpses of fly fisherman on the River Test. We visit the two Clatfords (meaning ford where the burdock grows) that straddle the River Anton. This ride also illustrates the vagaries of rural signposting in Hampshire, as mentioned elsewhere in this book. At many cross-roads there are often no signposts at all. At junctions that are signposted it is usually only in one direction and it always seems to be the direction that you have just come from. So you will have to follow the directions carefully if you are not to get lost. Short diversions from the route will take you to interesting local attractions like the Hawk Conservancy and the Army Flying Museum at Middle Wallop.

BACKGROUND AND PLACES OF INTEREST

Hawk Conservancy

The Hawk Conservancy was recently voted Visitor Attraction of the Year. There are opportunities to get hands-on experience of birds of prey in flight, and activity days when up to four people can spend time with the falconers and birds. The Hawk Conservancy has one of the largest collections of raptors (birds of prey) in the world. More than 200 birds can be seen in 9 hectares of grounds. Three times daily there are flying demonstrations and all the displays are different. Species such as owls, eagles, vultures, falcons, kites, hawks and secretary bird are incorporated into these displays. As it is a member of the National Federation of Zoos, the Hawk Conservancy is committed to conservation and breeding projects for rare species from around the world. As part of its aim to achieve an area of conservation, the grounds have evolved over a period of 33 years to give a natural woodland habitat and over 7 hectares have also been developed into a wild flower meadow. The wildlife can be observed or photographed from strategically placed viewing hides. A recently added attraction is the 'Vulture Restaurant' where visitors can see how these large birds interact with one another at feeding times. The Hawk Conservancy is open daily between February and October. (Tel: 01264 773850 for more information during office hours, or the 24-hour service on 01264 772252.)

The Museum of Army Flying

If you ride this route on a weekday, at most times there will be an army helicopter pilot in the air above you, from the School of Army Aviation at Middle Wallop, receiving flying training. Also situated at Middle Wallop base is the Museum of Army Flying in the Hayward

Hall, with its comprehensive history of British Army Aviation from the 1860s until the present day. The museum highlights the early flying pioneers and the Royal Flying Corps, Artillery Spotters, Airborne Forces and the Army Air Corps. There is an award-winning museum of military kites, gliders, aeroplanes and helicopters, with over 35 fixed and rotary wing aircraft. The collection of military gliders is the largest in Europe. As you wander around, you are able to follow the history of aviation from the earliest balloons and man-carrying kites, the development of airships and then to the Royal Flying Corps aeroplanes of World War 1. There are plenty of hands-on and interactive exhibits to enthral the younger members of the family. The army is justly proud of this collection of aircraft, imaginatively displayed in the purpose-built halls. The museum is open daily all the year round, except for Christmas week (tel: 01980 674421 for further information).

The Wallops

The three villages of Nether Wallop, Middle Wallop and Over Wallop lie along the Wallop Brook and derive their name from the Old English 'waella', which means stream, and 'hop', which means valley. The Wallops became famous during World War 2 when the air was full of the sound of Spitfires and Hurricanes taking off from the air stations during the Battle of Britain. The villages' more recent claim to fame was being featured as a backdrop for the popular TV series Miss Marple, but their history goes back much further than this. A settlement at Nether Wallop began in Norman times. The church of St Andrew is late Norman to Perpendicular and was enlarged in the 12th and 15th centuries. It has a fine west tower of flint dating from about 1704. Inside there are some interesting wall paintings urging Sunday observance, entitled 'A Warning to Sabbath Breakers'. The mural depicts Christ bleeding from wounds inflicted by people who work on Sundays. Cricket enthusiasts will find it interesting to note that some of the first cricket bats were made here by craftsmen using local willow; even W. G. Grace is reputed to have played with one. Over Wallop has a manor that was held by Godiva, wife of Leofric of Mercia, and it is thought that she might even have been born here.

Starting Point: This ride starts at the Danebury Hill Car Park.

Parking and Toilets: Park in the Danebury Hill Car Park about 3 miles northwest of Stockbridge. This is a free car park for visitors to the hill fort and toilets are provided.

Distance: 21.7 miles.

Maps: Ordnance Survey Landranger Sheets 184 and 185.

Hills: This ride takes place over undulating chalk downland and also visits some river valleys. There are no severe hills, but there are a number of short climbs.

Nature of Route: The ride follows surfaced roads, almost all of which are unclassified quiet country lanes.

Safety: There are no particular hazards associated with this route.

Refreshments: At just over 2 miles there is the Peat Spade Inn at Longstock. In Clatford (7 miles) there is the Clatford Arms, the Royal Oak and, a little further, the Crook and Shoes. In Monxton (11 miles) there is the Black Swan and at Grateley (14 miles) is the Plough Inn. Finally, the George Inn is situated on the A343 at Nether Wallop at a distance of 17 miles.

Nearest Tourist Information Centre: Town Mill House, Bridge Street, Andover, Hampshire SP10 1BL (tel: 01264 324320).

Cycle Hire: Behind the Bike Shed, 29 Charlton Road, Charlton, Andover, Hants (tel: 01264 338794). Boltons, 8 Andover Road, Ludgershall, Wilts (tel: 01264 791818).

Route Instructions:

1. (0.0 miles): From the Danebury Hill Car Park, cycle down the drive to the road and turn right.

2. (1.3 miles): At the crest of the hill, turn left down the narrow lane that is opposite the concrete farm buildings. This is known as Bottom Lane but is unmarked at this end. In typical Hampshire fashion there are no directions at this junction either.

3. (2.0 miles): At the end of Bottom Lane you will be close to the River Test — the first of

Above:
Danebury Hill.

ROUTE 12
A RIDE OF FOUR RIVERS
(A circular ride near Andover visiting the Rivers Test and Anton, and the Pilhill and Wallop Streams)

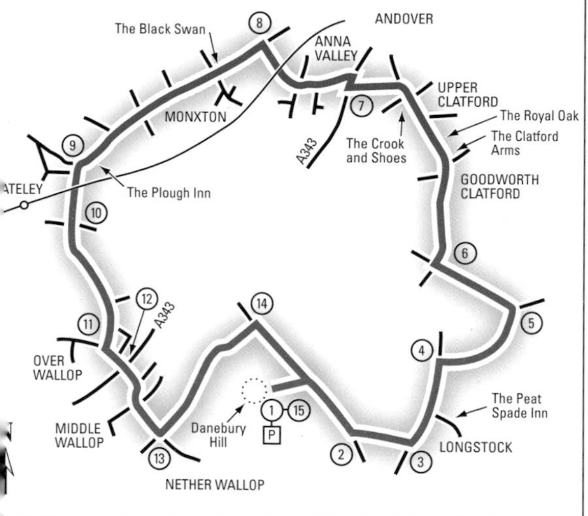

many watery scenes. Turn left here.

4. (3.2 miles): Take the narrow lane to the right that is marked 'Fullerton 2, Wherwell 3½'. This lane is lined with iron railings as it skirts the edge of Longstock House grounds.

5. (4.6 miles): At the three-way junction with a triangular grass island (the only sign is one telling you that you have just come from Longstock), turn left to cycle up the hill.

6. (5.9 miles): At the cross-roads, turn right as directed to 'The Clatfords 1, Andover 4'.

7. (9.7 miles): At the junction with the A343, carefully turn right and after about a hundred yards, turn left into Cattle Lane.

8. (10.9 miles): Just after passing under the railway viaduct there is a T-junction; turn left to enter the village of Monxton.

9. (14.2 miles): In the village of Grateley, turn left down the lane to Grateley House School.

10. (14.9 miles): At the crossroads, proceed straight on. Again the signposting tells you only that you have just come from Grateley. The lane that you should take has a sign indicating a width limit at 800yd ahead.

11. (16.5 miles): In Over Wallop, turn left by the war memorial.

12. (17.2 miles): At the junction with the A343 near the George Inn, cycle straight on as directed to Nether Wallop. You will be accompanied by the clear and fast flowing Wallop stream.

13. (18.3 miles): Take the unsignposted left turn by Gerrards Farm and Granary House to climb a steep hill.

14. (20.3 miles): You will come to a T-junction with no signpost and no identifying features at all. Turn right — soon you will recognise Danebury hill fort.

15. (21.7 miles): Arrive back at the car park.

ROUTE 13

THE NEW FOREST — BROCKENHURST AND BURLEY

(A circular ride taking in the Burley and Bolderwood Ornamental Drives)

The tree which moves some to tears of joy is in the eyes of others only a green thing that stands in the way. Some see nature all ridicule and deformity . . . and some scarce see nature at all. But to the eyes of the man of imagination, nature is imagination itself.
William Blake, 1798

This ride leaves Brockenhurst on the Rhinefield and Bolderwood Ornamental Drives. These are surfaced roads where ornamental tree species have been planted. The route then follows one of the main gravelled tracks of the New Forest down to Burley. From Burley we find the old railway line and follow this as far as the Old Station Tea Rooms, and then we wind our way back over unclassified roads to Brockenhurst. The New Forest is ideal for cycling due not only to the extensive off-road gravelled drives that are available but also to the 40mph speed limits on all the unfenced roads in the area. This is one of three rides that are based in the New Forest. Many parts of the forest are distinctly lacking in trees which is often a surprise to the first-time visitor, who might ask the question 'Where is the Forest?'. It is interesting to examine the meaning of the word 'forest'. To most people there is little question that it means a wood on a large scale, but it does not actually mean that at all; it means a royal property set apart as a sanctuary for wild animals. If the owner is not the Crown, it becomes a chase rather than a forest. Living within the boundaries of the forest are commoners. These are people that have certain rights that have accrued to them through the ownership of Forest property. The rights and the commoners' way of life have existed for more than nine centuries. There are rights of pasture where a commoner can graze a domestic animal in the open forest; the right of pannage or mast where it is permitted to turn out pigs in the autumn so that they can feed on acorns or beech mast; and fuelwood or estover which is the right to collect firewood.

BACKGROUND AND PLACES OF INTEREST

Brockenhurst

The New Forest villages have a character all of their own. Where else will you find ponies

Below:
On a forest track near Bolderwood.

Above:
An example of the excellent New Forest village waymarkers.

and cattle wandering freely through the streets and a ford called the Watersplash on the main road? And just outside the village, a cricket ground about half the size of a normal one built on a slope with several oak trees and a visiting mole within the playing area. Brockenhurst is truly at the heart of the New Forest and is set among some of the loveliest land in the area. It claims to have the oldest tree in the forest, which is a 1,000-year-old yew situated in the village churchyard.

Burley

A village that is very popular with coach tour operators, and is probably as typical a New Forest settlement as you can get. It is set in the middle of riding country with several stables and with access to miles of open heathland. Burley was at one time a notorious centre for smuggling and is renowned for its association with witches both in the past and present. It has a legend (no doubt encouraged by the local tourism association) — the Bisterne Dragon — which was supposed to come down from Burley Beacon for a daily drink of milk. The dragon was probably based on an outlaw or wild boar. The name of Dragon Lane still survives in the village.

The Rhinefield and Bolderwood Ornamental Drives

These drives form the heart of this ride and were formerly an old coaching route that ran between the A31 to the north and Brockenhurst. The Rhinefield Drive takes you through some huge conifers that were originally planted in 1859. One of the tallest types of conifer planted here is the Douglas Fir and some are already over 50m high. However, the tallest tree in the forest is the giant Wellingtonia that was planted in 1852 and has attained a height of 55m. This tree was named to commemorate the death of the Duke of Wellington and in its native California it can live for up to 3,400 years. Bolderwood Drive passes through ancient pollarded beeches at Mark Ash, and close to the A35 you will find the famous Knightwood Oak. This is believed to have been planted around 1600 and is one of the forest's largest pollarded oak trees. Several additional Royal commemorative oaks have been planted close by.

Beaulieu

Nearby is this charming village surrounded by woods and hills and situated on the Beaulieu River. In the grounds of Beaulieu are the ruined 13th century Abbey and Palace House. Here are many of the Montagu family treasures, including portraits and personal photographs. There is an exhibition of the monastic life of the Cistercians who founded the abbey in 1204. Of course many people visit Beaulieu for the splendid National Motor Museum. The exhibits date from the earliest examples of motoring to Damon Hill's Formula 1 championship-winning car. There are displays covering all aspects of the history of motoring, including a replica of a 1930s garage. There is also a large display of motorbikes and scooters and a gallery of commercial vehicles. The grounds of the abbey are full of interest with wonderful gardens and areas for picnics, and many free and unlimited rides. There is also a monorail that takes you through the roof of the motor museum. (For further information, tel: 01590 612123 or 01590 612345; web: www.beaulieu.co.uk.)

Starting Point: This ride starts from the Beachern Wood Car Park — see below.

Parking and Toilets: Car parks and picnic sites are well provided in the New Forest and there is a plentiful selection around the route on the Rhinefield and Bolderwood Ornamental Drives, and in Burley and Brockenhurst. My

Above:
New Forest ponies.

choice was to park near Brockenhurst in the Beachern Wood Car Park. This is on the northwest edge of Brockenhurst on the Rhinefield Ornamental Drive. Some of the picnic sites have toilets — Bolderwood is one of these.

Travel by Rail: It is perfectly feasible to travel to the start of this ride by train. Brockenhurst is on the main Waterloo to Weymouth line. For details of carriage of cycles on this line, please refer to the 'Transporting Cycles' section.

Distance: 20.6 miles.

Maps: Ordnance Survey Landranger Sheets 195 and 196.

Hills: There is the occasional short but steep climb.

Nature of Route: The initial section of this ride, on the ornamental drives, has been approved by Hampshire County Council as a suitable route for cyclists. After this, there is a significant amount of easy off-road mileage (about 4 miles is on the gravelled track that links Minstead to Burley and a further 2 miles on the old railway track that links Burbush to Wilverley). The rest of the route is on quiet, unclassified country roads.

Safety: On some of the New Forest roads (for example the Rhinefield Ornamental Drive) there can be a significant camber, making the road edge difficult to use. Although not a serious hazard, young or inexperienced riders should take care. Also, you should remember that the New Forest is a working forest and off-road cycle routes could change at short notice. If you come across timber operations on your ride, stop and dismount and do not proceed until the operator has signalled that he is aware of your presence, then walk with your cycle until you are clear of all machinery. It is also perhaps worth mentioning that adders are common in the New Forest although the chances of receiving a bite are extremely remote.

Refreshments: The Queens Head and others in Burley (11 miles). The Station Tea Rooms

(15 miles) and several places in Brockenhurst at the start and end of the ride.

Nearest Tourist Information Centre: New Forest Museum and Visitor Centre, Main Car Park, Lyndhurst, Hampshire SO43 7NY (tel: 023 8028 2269).

Cycle Hire: Please refer to the list of New Forest cycle hire outlets in the 'Useful Addresses' chapter.

Supplementary Information: *Cycling in the New Forest — The Network Map* is a useful guide to the gravelled tracks and recommended road routes that form the New Forest Cycle Network. It contains a map of the network and the waymarking system is explained. It is inexpensive and is available from the New Forest Visitor Centre — see above. A pre-recorded Forestry Commission information line contains regularly updated information about forthcoming events, guided walks and timber operations (tel: 023 8028 4476).

Route Instructions:

1. (0.0 miles): Leave the Beachern Wood Car Park by turning right on to the Rhinefield Ornamental Drive.

2. (3.4 miles): The Rhinefield Ornamental Drive meets the A35. Take care here as it is a busy road — it is probably best to dismount — and go straight across. Carry on in the same direction; this road is the Bolderwood Ornamental Drive.

3. (6.3 miles): Bear left on the road signposted 'Fritham 5, Linwood 4'.

4. (6.5 miles): Take the gravelled track off to the left indicated by the Waymarker Post No 12 and marked 'Burley 5 miles'. Keep following the gravelled track waymarker posts with the white arrows (see example in photograph) for several miles until you reach Waymarker Post No 9.

5. (10.2 miles): At Waymarker Post No 9 turn right on to the surfaced road that takes you into Burley village.

6. (11.1 miles): When you leave Chapel Lane (by the Queens Head), take the road signposted 'Ringwood' and cycle through Burley.

7. (11.7 miles): There is a left turn opposite Burley Bike Hire, turn here as signposted to 'Bransgore, Christchurch and Avon Tyrrell'.

8. (12.7 miles): Turn left into Burbush Hill Car Park and descend to the cutting where you will find the old railway line and follow it east (left). Continue on the line, crossing the occasional road and track until you reach its end at the Old Station Tea Rooms.

9. (14.8 miles): Leave the old track by the gate that gives you access to the road and then take the road under the bridge (the Old Station Tea Rooms will be on your right).

10. (19.2 miles): As you approach Brockenhurst all you need to do, if you are returning to your starting point, is to keep on this road (following signs to Rhinefield) and avoid right turns into the town. The road skirts the edge of Brockenhurst and leads you back to Beachern Wood Car Park.

11. (20.6 miles): Arrive back at the car park.

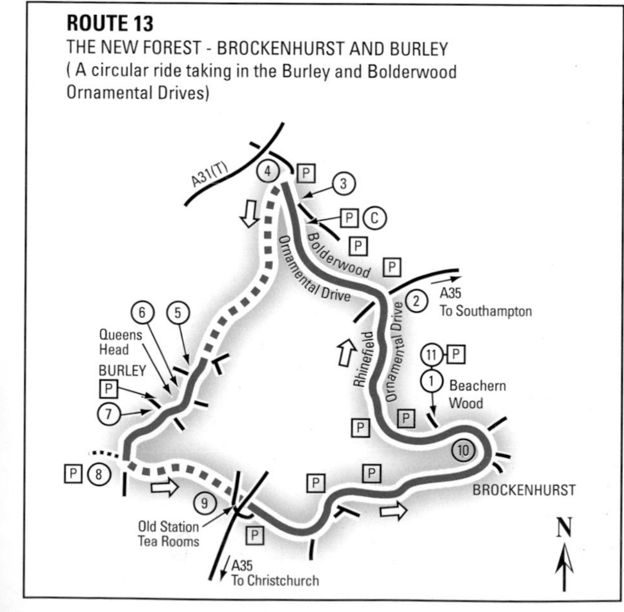

Left: Barren but beautiful heathland near Frogham.

THE NEW FOREST — FRITHAM AND FROGHAM AND BACK THROUGH LINWOOD

(A circular ride in the quieter part of the forest)

Forests afford so much plunder of different kinds, especially in deer stealing, lopping timber, and poaching that the neighbouring parishes are much tainted with idleness, dissipation and dishonesty.

From a statement in 1804 by the Rev William Gilpin giving his reasons for his generous provision of a school for the village of Boldre

The New Forest is bisected by the A31 that runs from Southampton to Ringwood. In my view, the area of the forest to the northwest of this trunk road is the most enjoyable as it is much less frequented by tourists and holiday-makers than the area to the southeast which includes Beaulieu, Lyndhurst and Brockenhurst. This circular ride is routed over a combination of gravelled tracks and quiet lanes, and is relatively traffic-free. Place names of an area have always had a particular interest for me and certain New Forest place names recur regularly and have a character all of their own. For example, wherever you see the word 'holm' starting in a place name it indicates an area of holly trees — examples are Holmhill and Holmsley. You will also occasionally see 'hat' which means a stand of trees elevated on a small hill — one example being 'Standing Hat'. If 'ley' occurs at the end of a place name it indicates a clearing, and 'bur' is derived from 'burgh' meaning a hill or fort. Finally, wherever 'hart' occurs it indicates a place associated at one time with a red deer stag — a Royal beast of the Norman hunting forest.

BACKGROUND AND PLACES OF INTEREST

Fritham

Fritham is a quiet little village — one might possibly say a typical New Forest settlement of commoners where the people still exercise their ancient Forest Rights, putting their ponies out to graze and their pigs out for pannage. The village pub (the Royal Oak) is a particular delight for the enthusiast who searches out remote country pubs: no chromium, no music, no fitted carpets, no hot food, beer in wooden barrels and a characterful proprietor. When you cross the threshold it is like stepping into a pub of 30 years ago. There are two basic bars, one with high-backed settles and chairs, and pots and kettles hanging in a wide old chimney. There are outside seats and to keep you company outside there will probably be friendly sheep, cows, pigs or ponies wandering nearby.

Stoney Cross Airfield

You may notice that the road approaching Stoney Cross, across Ocknell Plain, is very flat and has concrete pads spaced along the verge. This is because the road follows one of the runways of Stoney Cross Airfield, which was built in 1942 and was one of the three main airfields built in the forest in the war to support the D-Day landings.

The Schultze Gunpowder Factory

Close to the point where you pick up the cycle track, you may see a plaque commemorating this factory. Although there is no sign of it now, about a hundred years ago this New Forest factory employed 100 people in 70 buildings. The directors claimed that it was the premier nitro-compound gunpowder factory in the world. The company's reputation was made with the hunting community of the time for its smokeless powder.

Starting Point: This ride starts at Fritham Car Park (see below).

Parking and Toilets: Fritham Car Park is as good a place as any to start this ride. There are many other car parks dotted around this route and the locations of some of these are shown on the sketch map.

Distance: 16.2 miles.

Map: Ordnance Survey Landranger Sheet 195.

Hills: This is a largely flat ride with a small number of hills. There is a steep ascent on the forest track section at 1½ miles and a significant climb through Rockford Common. Otherwise the going is easy, with the section south through the Avon Valley being particularly flat and enjoyable.

Nature of Route: This ride starts off with four entirely traffic-free miles on a forest track. Next there is a very pleasant section that follows the course of the Avon Valley between Frogham and Mockbeggar and is consequently very flat. The final leg is on high, flat, and usually open gorse-covered heathland.

Safety: There are no particular hazards associated with this ride. In common with the rest of the forest, traffic on some of the roads is likely to be significant on Bank Holidays so the ride is likely to be more enjoyable if these days are avoided.

Refreshments: The Foresters Arms is at Hyde at 4 miles. The Royal Oak and the North Gorley Tea Rooms are at just over 5 miles. The Red Shoot Inn at Linwood is at 9 miles and, finally, the High Corner Inn is situated just off the route at about 10 miles.

Nearest Tourist Information Centre: The Furlong, Ringwood, Hampshire BH24 1AZ (tel: 01425 470896).

Cycle Hire: Please refer to the list of New Forest cycle hire outlets in the 'Useful Addresses' chapter.

Route Instructions:

1. (0.0 miles): From the Fritham Car Park close to the village, you need to be careful to ensure that you find the correct track. It is not the most obvious one, that continues in the same direction that you entered the car park through the barrier to Fritham Plain (this is not a cycle track). Instead, turn back towards the entrance to the car park and locate the track labelled with the cycle logo.

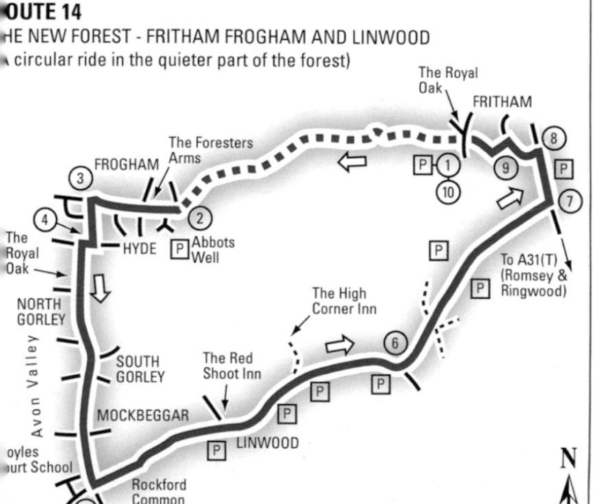

2. (3.7 miles): The gravelled track ends at Abbots Well, where it meets a country lane on a hairpin bend. Continue in the same direction, up the hill, with a white house and a tiny pink 'toy house' on the right. This road continues through Hyde past the Foresters Arms and the Hyde Memorial Hall and then through Frogham.

3. (4.8 miles): Turn left at Hyde Lane. There is a nearly illegible signpost that seems to say 'North Gorley 1, Ringwood 6'. This road skirts the edge of the New Forest.

4. (5.3 miles): At the end of Hyde Lane, turn right then immediately left as directed to North Gorley ½, Ringwoood 6'.

5. (8.0 miles): Just after passing through Mockbeggar, cross the ford and take the

left turn to Linwood (also signposted to the Red Shoot Inn and the High Corner Inn). You will pass through Linwood and then on to very open gorse-covered heathland.

6. (12.1 miles): Turn left as directed to Stoney Cross.

7. (14.7 miles): At Stoney Cross give-way junction, turn left to head north. There was no signpost at the time of riding, except one that tells you that you have just come from Linwood and Bolderwood.

8. (15.2 miles): Turn left back toward Fritham. At the time of riding, there was no signpost here. The only identifying feature being a 'Feeding of Animals prohibited' sign.

9. (15.6 miles): Turn left opposite some old derelict farm buildings. Again there was no signpost at the time of my ride.

10. (16.2 miles): Arrive in Fritham; the car park is a little beyond the Royal Oak.

Above:
Happy times on the New Forest tracks.

Below:
The Red Shoot Inn at Linwood.

THE NEW FOREST — LINWOOD AND LINFORD

(A short circular route on forest tracks around Linwood)

For never have I known any human habitation, in a land where people are discovered dwelling in so many secret, green, out-of-the-world places, which had so much of nature in and about it.
W. H. Hudson writing about the New Forest in his *Hampshire Days*, published in 1903

Above:
Linford Bottom.

This ride is the shortest one in this book, and one of three set in the New Forest. It is a circular route that takes you clockwise from Linwood and then parallel with the A31 across Bratley Plain to Picket Post and then back to Linwood. It is a short route of only 10 miles that is almost completely off-road on permissive forest tracks authorised for cycling, with the exception of two very short stretches. This makes it a very suitable ride for children. The ride takes place in a good mix of woodland and also sandy heathland.

BACKGROUND AND PLACES OF INTEREST

Fordingbridge

Six miles northwest of Linwood, situated in Hampshire near the Dorset border, this town cannot really make up its mind to which county it belongs. It is a picturesque place with its medieval bridge of seven arches which spans the River Avon that has made it such an important crossing point. Its buildings are comparatively young, mostly built in the 19th century due to a large fire that destroyed the old town. Augustus John loved Fordingbridge and did a great deal of painting there. Close to the bridge there is a bronze statue erected in his memory. At nearby North Gorley is the old oak tree that Charles II is reputed to have hidden in for several days to escape the clutches of the Roundheads. Fordingbridge is perhaps now best known for being the headquarters of those who come to find trout in the nearby trout streams. Although the River Avon cannot compete with the other Hampshire rivers for trout, it has the best coarse fishing the county has to offer.

The Rufus Stone

This memorial, at Castle Malwood Walk, Minstead, is just a few miles from the ride. It commemorates an oak tree that was responsible for the death of William Rufus (King William II) on 2 August 1100. There are many accounts of what actually happened and it is not really known whether the king's death was by accident or design. The stone itself recounts that one of the king's hunting partners (Sir Walter Tyrrell) shot an arrow at a stag but it glanced off the tree and hit King William in the chest and he died instantly. The king was very unpopular with the clergy and the people, and the question will always remain as to whether or not it was murder, especially as the whole hunting party immediately fled. Sir Walter went to Normandy where even on his death bed he denied responsibility and the king's brother immediately galloped to Winchester to be proclaimed king. Furthermore, the body was left where it fell until it was picked up by a charcoal burner and conveyed to Winchester in his cart

Starting Point: This ride starts from the Appleslade Walkers Car Park — see below.

Parking and Toilets: I parked in the Appleslade Walkers Car Park, about ½ mile west of Linwood. An alternative parking and starting place is the car park at Linford Bottom. Both of these sites are very attractive spots for picnics, especially Linford Bottom where you can sit beside an attractive stream.

Distance: 9.6 miles.

Map: Ordnance Survey Landranger Sheet 195.

Hills: There is only one long climb on this ride (at Linford Bottom Car Park). There are a few short climbs after leaving the track that is parallel with the A31.

Nature of Route: This ride is short and is almost entirely on forest tracks. It is therefore suitable for young children. The tracks from Route Instructions 2 to 4 and from 10 to 11 are excellent and make good cycling. The track parallel with the A31 is of lesser quality. In some places it has virtually no gravel surface and can become waterlogged at times, but is still comfortably cyclable.

Safety: Be careful when going downhill on gravelled forest tracks as patches of loose gravel can mean that you lose control of your steering.

Refreshments: In Linwood itself there is the excellent Red Shoot Inn — this can be very busy on Sundays and Bank Holidays.

Nearest Tourist Information Centre: The Furlong, Ringwood, Hampshire BH24 1AZ (tel: 01425 470896).

Cycle Hire: Please refer to the list of New Forest cycle hire outlets in the 'Useful Addresses' chapter.

Route Instructions:

Note: Sections of the ride are routed over gravelled cycle tracks. These tracks are all waymarked with green and white plastic waymarkers on wooden posts. Some of the waymarker posts are also numbered to aid navigation, and I have referred to these where necessary.

1. (0.0 miles): From the car park at Appleslade, turn right to climb past the Red Shoot Inn and through the hamlet of Linwood.

2. (0.5 miles): Where the road swings sharply left, turn right on to the gravelled track as indicated by the cycling waymarker. After about 200yd you will pass through a forest gate by a white cottage.

3. (0.8 miles): You will meet a choice of gravelled tracks (at Cycling Waymarker No 5); avoid the left option and continue straight on up the hill. Continue on the track through the occasional gate and past a number of cycling waymarkers.

4. (2.1 miles): At Cycling Waymarker No 7 turn right to head towards the busy A31 road in the distance, and then cycle close and parallel to it.

5. (3.0 miles): The track forks and the direction of the cycling waymarker is slightly ambiguous. You will need to take the left option to continue cycling parallel with the A31.

6. (4.3 miles): Turn right, away from the A31 as indicated by the cycling waymarker and then sharp left as indicated by a further cycling waymarker to continue parallel with the A31.

7. (4.5 miles): At Cycling Waymarker No 8 descend a short steep hill, and then turn right, away from the small underpass under the A31 to continue following the cycle track.

8. (5.2 miles): The cycle track meets a narrow surfaced road opposite the drive to Broomy House. Turn right here.

9. (5.6 miles): Turn right on the drive to Linford Bottom Car Park and pass over the small bridge over the stream. Do not turn right into the car park, but carry on up the hill where it says 'Access to private properties only'.

10. (5.9 miles): When the surfaced road peters out you will need to take the cycle track on the right as indicated by the cycling waymarker. This diverges to the right, away from the drive to Waterslade Farm. Continue on the cycle track past various cycling waymarkers and gates.

11. (8.1 miles): At the T-junction, identified by Cycling Waymarker No 6, turn left. You will recognise that you are now retracing your outward route and you merely need to follow this back to the starting point.

12. (9.6 miles): Arrive back at Appleslade Walkers Car Park.

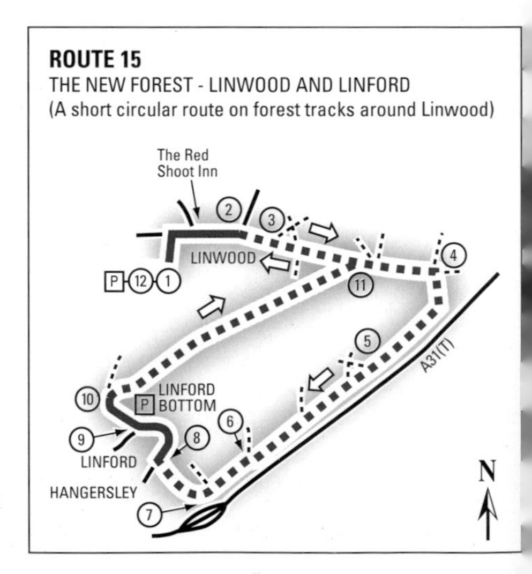

THE AVON VALLEY — FORDINGBRIDGE TO DOWNTON

(A circular ride following both sides of the Avon Valley)

. . . Yon heathy hill
That rises sudden from the vale so green,
The vale far stretching as the view can reach
Under its long dark ridge, the river here
That, like a serpent, through the grassy mead
Winds on.

From *For the Banks of the Hampshire Avon* by Robert Southey

Above:
A village scene near Breamore.

The outward leg of this ride takes a pleasant route on the west side of the river and then very gradually climbs through Whitsbury and then on to Wick Down. This is horse-training country with sizeable stables in Whitsbury and areas of the down set aside for gallops. The route then drops down into the Avon Valley to Downton and runs between the east bank of the river and the edge of the New Forest before returning to Fordingbridge. The section of the ride that runs across Wick Down is on rights of way classified as RUPPs (Roads Used as Public Paths) and the surface of them is in a poor state. I spent some time talking to a farm-worker on Wick Down and learnt that this is due to erosion by four-wheel drive vehicles. I rode the route after very wet weather and some sections were flooded to a depth of several inches and it was difficult to pass without getting wet feet. A very limited effort has been made by one of the four-wheel drive clubs to provide a causeway for walkers and cyclists but the severity of the damage means that it is largely ineffective. If you are planning to cycle the route after wet weather then be ready to experience wet feet and clothes. Otherwise, this is a glorious ride that I am sure you will enjoy.

BACKGROUND AND PLACES OF INTEREST

Fordingbridge

[see Route 15]

Downton

The medieval borough of Downton is an attractive settlement consisting of two rows of houses that are mostly brick and thatch. These line a wide street with a strip of grass down its centre. The village is divided by the River Avon and the centre is dominated by an old tannery, built in 1918, with its frontage on the river bank. I spent some time eating my packed lunch on the bridge and it was such a peaceful scene watching the clear fast-flowing water pass underneath, the swans gliding by, and the yellow wagtails flitting here and there. I fell into conversation with an old man who was passing by and I asked him what it was like to live in such a beautiful place. He said that he had lived in Downton all of his life and he loved it, but they have lots of visitors and there is nothing for them to do, unless they like fishing. In recent times, Downton, like Fordingbridge has become an angling centre for the Avon and also its neighbouring chalk streams, the Wylye, Nadder and Ebble. The 300-hundred-year old Bull Hotel has attracted anglers since prewar days, and its walls are hung with fine specimens of trout, pike and perch.

Breamore House and Village

Breamore, or 'Bremmer' as the locals call it, is a historic, unspoilt 17th century village that lies very close to the ride. It has a manor house, many thatched cottages and a common. The Breamore Countryside Museum concentrates on the period when the village was self-sufficient and replicas of a farm worker's cottage, a blacksmith's shop, a dairy, a wheelwright's works, a brewery, a saddler's shop and a cobbler's shed are there to be viewed. The manor house itself was completed by the Dodington family in 1583. It was bought in the early 18th century by Sir Edward Hulse. It is still occupied by his descendants and remains their family home. There is a fine collection of paintings, period furniture, needlework, porcelain and many other items of interest. The museum and house are open in the afternoon at Easter and from April to September on a variable number of days per month (tel: 01725 512468 or 512233 for more information).

Above:
A timber-framed cottage on the route.

Hills: On the outward leg there are some short hills as you climb on to the downs, but nothing serious. The return leg is flat as it follows close to the river.

Nature of Route: This ride takes place almost entirely on unclassified country lanes, apart from one section of about 2 miles on a bridleway and RUPPs. Unfortunately, the RUPPs have been severely damaged by four-wheel drive vehicles and can be heavy going in wet weather. Expect to get wet and muddy on this section if the weather has been wet.

Starting Point: This ride starts from the A338 slip road car park in Fordingbridge (see below).

Parking and Toilets: Park in Fordingbridge in the A338 slip road car park. This is situated at the southeast corner of Fordingbridge and is sandwiched between the A338 and its slip road. It is a long-stay car park and is therefore inexpensive. Be careful if you carry your cycles on a roof bar carrier as the car park entrance is fitted with a height restriction bar. There are public conveniences in Fordingbridge. Car parks are also available in Downton. The latter part of the ride skirts the edge of the New Forest and there are several car parks along the route that you could use between Woodgreen and Godshill.

Distance: 17.0 miles.

Maps: Ordnance Survey Landranger Sheets 184 and 195.

Safety: There are no particular safety hazards associated with this ride.

Refreshments: There are a number of pubs around the route. There is the Cartwheel free house. The Bull, White Horse, Kings Arms and Wooden Spoon in Downton, and the Horse and Groom at Woodgreen. Lastly, there is the nice-looking Fighting Cocks in Godshill.

Nearest Tourist Information Centre: (Open Easter to September only) Kings Yard, Salisbury Street, Fordingbridge, Hampshire SP6 1AB (tel: 01425 654560).

Cycle Hire: Perkins Cycle Hire, 11 Provost Street, Fordingbridge, Hampshire SP6 1AY (tel: 01425 653475).

Route Instructions:

1. (0.0 miles): Emerge from the A338 slip-road

car park in Fordingbridge by turning right and continuing along the slip road. Then turn left into Bridge Street, cross the bridge and turn right at the mini-roundabout.

2. (0.4 miles): Turn left into Park Road and then, at the end of the road, turn right into Whitsbury Road (no visible sign at this point). You will soon find yourself in pleasant countryside.

3. (1.2 miles): At the point where the road turns sharp left, turn right down a narrow lane signposted to Breamore.

4. (1.6 miles): At the junction by the post office letterbox, instead of swinging right, continue straight ahead on a narrow road (there were no directions at the time of riding).

5. (2.9 miles): Turn left as signposted for Whitsbury.

6. (3.8 miles): After climbing the steep hill through the wood, turn right as signposted 'Whitsbury ¾'.

7. (4.2 miles): After descending a steep hill you will come to a give-way junction; take the route signposted to Whitsbury again.

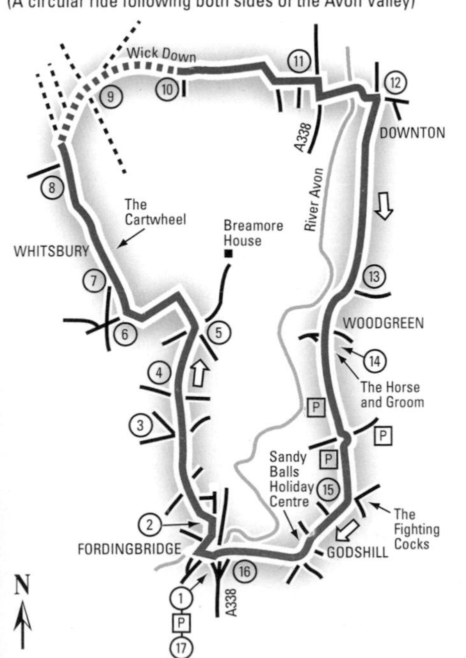

8. (5.5 miles): Where the road swings left to Rockbourne, carry straight on (the road becomes unsurfaced at this point). You will soon meet a junction of byways — take the right-hand one of the two, which effectively means you turn half right to pass the wooden barn with the tin roof. Shortly after this you take the right of two possible routes and this is provided with a separate parallel pathway for horses and cycles to replace the track damaged by four-wheel drive vehicles.

9. (6.2 miles): There is a further junction of byways. You go straight on here and this junction is only mentioned because at this point the track can be very wet in most seasons and very wide due to over-use by four-wheel drive vehicles. There is an elevated path on the left, to get through the mire, constructed by one of the four-wheel drive associations, presumably in mitigation for the damage caused. At the end of the very wide track, take the right-hand of the two routes that takes you on to Wick Down.

10. (7.9 miles): Rejoin the surfaced road, and enjoy a longish downhill run into Downton.

11. (9.5 miles): At the junction with the A338 by the Downton cross-roads post office, turn right on to the A338, and then left at the traffic lights toward the village centre.

12. (10.4 miles): In the village, turn right as directed to the Moot Landscape Garden.

13. (12.5 miles): At the end of Moot Lane, turn right as directed to Woodgreen and Breamore.

14. (13.1 miles): Swing left for 'Godshill 2, via ford'.

15. (15.0 miles): At the give-way junction in Godshill, turn right as directed to 'B3078 Fordingbridge 2'; this is also known as the Roger Penny Way.

16. (16.9 miles): On return to Fordingbridge, pass under the concrete bridge that carries the A338 and then take the next left to return to the car park.

17. (17.0 miles): Arrive back at the car park.

THE AVON VALLEY — RINGWOOD TO THE SEA

(A ride down the Avon Valley from Ringwood to Mudeford)

Mudeford bid fair at one time to be a popular seaside resort; but fashion forsook its little lodging-houses for the new villas in the young pine woods on the sandy cliffs to the west.

D. H. Moutray Read writing about Mudeford in his *Highways and Byways in Hampshire*

This ride heads due south along the Avon Valley from Ringwood toward the sea and is never more than a couple of miles from the river. It continues our progression along the River Avon from Route No 16, where we explored from Downton to Fordingbridge, and Route No 14, where we cycled between the western edge of the New Forest and the Avon Valley. The route utilises some very quiet, unclassified country lanes almost all of the way to Christchurch, and provides some very peaceful and relaxed cycling. Crossing the busy A35 dual carriageway is not as hazardous as I imagined it would be, due to the footbridge that has been provided connecting Salisbury Road with Burton Road. From there to Mudeford it is only a short distance on urban roads. My original plan for this ride was to return to Ringwood using the B3347. Unfortunately, I found this road to be busier than I expected and the traffic fast moving. For family cycling — especially if you have young children — I would therefore recommend returning along the same course as your outward route.

Above:
Mudeford

BACKGROUND AND PLACES OF INTEREST

Ringwood

Ringwood has been the main town of the New Forest for centuries. In Saxon times it had a royal manor, with a church and hall and in the 13th century a 'new' church was built but this was pulled down and then rebuilt over 100 years ago. In 1226 Ringwood was given a market charter and, although now much smaller, it still holds a weekly morning market on a Wednesday. The town itself has remained reasonably unspoilt. There are quaint and modern shops, street entertainment, restaurants, cafés and pubs. There is not a great deal of historical interest in the town other than the attractive manor house. However, it is said that the Duke of Monmouth wrote to his uncle, James II, in a house in West Street by the old three-arched stone bridge that crosses the River Avon, and now called Monmouth House. His letter was a cowardly appeal begging for mercy. Ringwood's breweries have always been renowned, but only one remains. A gardener by the name of Bower was reputed to drink 16 pints of Ringwood ale a day while working in the churchyard! The sexton, it was noted, was allowed only half that quantity! The Lamb Inn was built to serve as a railway station for the Ringwood spur line but, when the line was completed, they discovered it had been built in the wrong place and should have been some quarter of a mile away! So the station was never used and it was eventually made into the Lamb Inn. The man responsible for this gross error was Castleman and ever since the day the railway opened it has been

Above:
Mudeford Quay.

nicknamed ‘Castleman’s Corkscrew’, due to its twisting nature. The new line later became redundant and the station pulled down.

Christchurch and Mudeford

Christchurch takes its name from the 11th century priory that dominates the town. The Priory Church is the longest parish church in England and was originally known as Christ’s Church at Twynham. The castle too was once known as Twynham Castle but the Twynham was later dropped and for many centuries now the ancient borough has simply been called Christchurch. Little of the 12th century castle remains except sections of the massive walls of the keep on an artificial mound. These ruins, along with the ruins of Constable’s House beside the Mill Stream, are now in the care of English Heritage and open to the public. Much of the older part of Christchurch has retained its historic charm. There are old buildings and quaint shops as well as more modern shops, restaurants, cafés and public houses. Museums include the Red House Museum in Quay Road and the Southern Electric Museum housed in the old power station at Bargates. There is also Place Mill which displays work by local artists and crafts people. Within Christchurch are several gardens and open spaces to walk around. Convent Walk was opened in 1911 to commemorate the coronation of King George V. On this walk can be seen excellent views of the Priory Church and Gardens and also the quay. At the quay the rivers Stour and Avon meet and flow into the harbour. The beaches at Christchurch are very good and uncommercialised. Boats can be hired to Hengistbury Head. At the eastern end is Mudeford sandbank, a strip of duneland and beach which is completely inaccessible to cars and so has a delightful, peaceful and relaxed atmosphere.

Moors Valley Country Park and Forest

The park is situated only about 3 miles west of Ringwood and occupies an area of 300 hectares in the valley of the Moors River. There are several cycle paths providing traffic-free cycling routes of up to 6 miles. The visitor centre is housed in an 18th century timber barn and contains a cycle hire outlet (see ‘Cycle Hire’ below). There are several play areas for young children, a narrow gauge steam railway and an 18-hole golf course. Moors Valley is open every day from 7.00am until dusk. There are no admission charges but parking charges apply. For further information contact the Information Point and Wardens’ Office (tel: 01425 470721).

Starting Point: This ride starts from the Market Place Car Park in Ringwood (see below).

Parking and Toilets: Parking in Ringwood is not an easy task — I could find only two car parks and these do not seem to be adequate. Also, they are constricted with a separate entrance and exit, and anyone wishing to park is forced to drive nose to tail around a single route. Consequently, at busy times it can take an age to get into and out of the car parks. I parked in the Market Place Car Park — make sure that you park in the long-stay section as there is a three-hour restriction on short-stay parking. However, to be fair to the town, there is no charge for parking. Access to the car park is via Christchurch Road (entrance by the Methodist Church). If you prefer, you could start from Mudeford in which case you will need to park at the Mudeford Quay Car Park.

Distance: 19.9 miles.

Map: Ordnance Survey Landranger Sheet 195.

Hills: This is an extremely flat ride with no significant hills.

Nature of Route: The outward leg of this ride follows a very quiet and flat set of country lanes, almost to Christchurch. The B3347 may be used for the return leg, but although it has the advantage of following the River Avon closely, it is rather busy at times.

Safety: If you decide to return on the B3347, care should be taken on the A35 roundabout which is very busy and fast.

Refreshments: There is a large choice of places in Ringwood. In the countryside there is the Lamb Inn at Winkton. The Manor Arms is a few yards from the route at Burton. In Christchurch there is the Ship in Distress, Café 39 and the Nelson Tavern. At Mudeford, on the quay, there is the Haven House Inn and Haven Café. On the return journey there is the Fishermans Haunt, just south of Sopley. In Sopley there is the Woolpack and the New Queen in Avon

Nearest Tourist Information Centre: The Furlong, Ringwood, Hampshire BH24 1AZ (tel: 01425 470896).

Cycle Hire: There is a cycle hire facility about 3 miles west of Ringwood at Moors Valley Country Park, Horton Road, Ashley Heath, Ringwood, Hants BH24 2ET
(tel: 01425 470721).

Route Instructions:

1. (0.0 miles): Leave the Market Place Car Park in Ringwood, swing left and then left again into Bickerley Road which runs along the edge of Bickerley Common. At the small roundabout turn right as directed to Sopley and Winkton on the B3347.

2. (1.0 miles): Turn left on the road signposted to Burley 4¼ and then immediately right as signposted to Ringwood Town football ground.

Below:
The church of St Peter and St Paul, Ringwood.

3. (3.6 miles): Take a right turn as directed to North Ripley.

4. (5.9 miles): At the slightly staggered cross-roads (no signpost) proceed straight on along the narrow lane — this has a 6ft 6in access limitation.

5. (6.5 miles): At the Winkton Junction — within sight of the Lamb Inn — turn right here to leave Harpway Lane to join Burley Road and then left into Bockhampton Road.

6. (6.8 miles): Turn right into Tinyard Lane (very narrow).

7. (7.3 miles): At a red-brick cottage known as Hawthorn Farm Cottage, turn right and almost immediately turn right again to continue along Hawthorn Road.

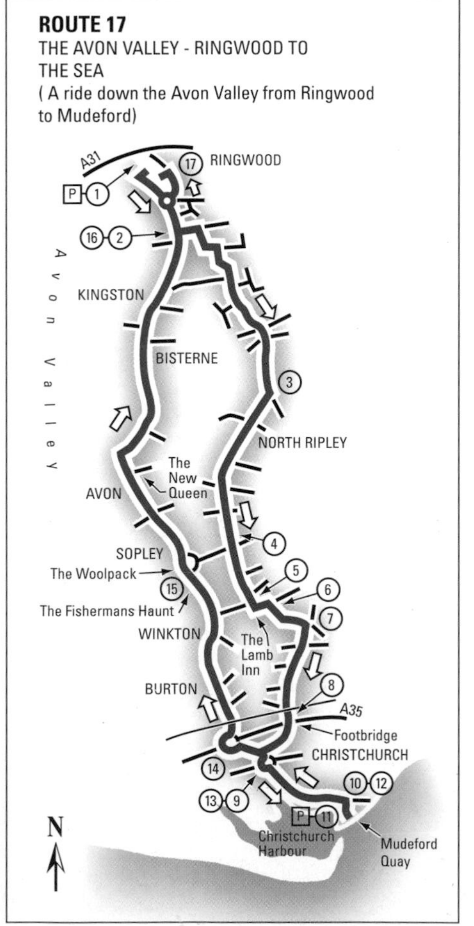

8. (8.7 miles): After passing under the railway bridge, Hawthorn Road emerges into Salisbury Road. This in turn meets the very busy and fast A35. Use the steel pedestrian bridge to cross the A35 and to deliver you safely to the other side. Cycle along Burton Road — you will need to do one left turn to stay on Burton Road. At the end of Burton Road, you will need to dismount (it is a no through road) and walk the short distance to the roundabout.

9. (9.1 miles): At the roundabout carry straight on into Stanpit and continue on this road.

10. (10.2 miles): Turn right into Chichester Way for Mudeford Quay.

11. (10.5 miles): Arrive at Mudeford Quay and enjoy the sea air.

If you wish to return to Ringwood by a different route, using the B3347, then follow the remaining directions. If not, then merely retrace your outward route.

12. (10.8 miles): Leave Chichester Way by turning left and cycling along Stanpit.

13. (11.9 miles): At the roundabout, go straight on into Purewell Cross Road.

14. (12.2 miles): Negotiate the A35 roundabout and take the B3347 exit into Stony Lane, signposted Burton, Winkton and Sopley. (Take great care here as this is a large and busy roundabout.)

15. (14.5 miles): In Sopley, you will need to turn left by the Woolpack to enter the small one-way system.

16. (19.5 miles): In Ringwood you will meet a small roundabout where you go straight on as directed to the town centre, then turn left by the war memorial and then left into the car park entrance by the Methodist Church.

17. (19.9 miles): Arrive back at the Market Place Car Park.

THE ISLE OF PURBECK

(A circular ride along the heathland bridleways and winding lanes around Studland)

There is no definite hamlet, no village street, no centre, no beginning, no end. It is merely a casual, unarranged sample of rural Dorset brought, in all its luxuriant greenness, to the very water's edge.

Sir Frederick Treves writing about the village of Studland in his *Highways and Byways in Dorset*

The early part of this ride takes you across the heart of Studland Heath and you realise what a very special habitat heathland is. There is not very much of it left in this country and a significant part of what remains is in Dorset. It is a strikingly different habitat, caused by underlying poor and usually sandy soil which is acidic in nature and leads to the proliferation of plants such as heather. The soil is also unable to support trees of significant size and consequently the land has a comparatively barren appearance. These characteristics bring their own bird and animal life with them too. Rare sand lizards and the smooth snake (non-poisonous) are often seen and the comparatively rare Dartford warbler and stonechat can usually be found. The hobby and nightjar are occasional visitors. The heath also abounds with many types of dragonfly, damselfly and butterfly. I cycled the route in mid-June and I have never seen so much honeysuckle draping the English hedgerows as I saw then. The other treat was the orchids growing in the damper parts of the heath. They were fine examples and a completely unexpected delight. The return leg from Corfe to the outskirts of Swanage is also very pleasant. This uses a lane that serves the farms and fields on the flank of Brenscombe Hill and Nine Barrow Down. Every so often in the valley below, you will hear the whistle and see the steam of the trains of the Swanage Railway as they ply their way back and forth between Swanage and Corfe Castle.

BACKGROUND AND PLACES OF INTEREST

The Isle of Purbeck

It is not an island at all, of course, as it has water on only three sides, and in fact it has never been an island. The only way that it could come close to being considered as such, is that it has a feel all of its own — so very different from the rest of Dorset. It is of course famous for its stone and there has been a considerable history of quarrying in the area. Most people will have heard of Purbeck marble, which has been quarried and shipped

Below:
A view of Studland Heath.

from Swanage for Exeter, Lincoln and Salisbury cathedrals as well as many of the cathedrals of Europe.

Corfe Castle

The castle is an extremely picturesque ruin and its position is second to none. Across the Isle of Purbeck running east to west lie the Purbeck Hills and these form a high ridge of downland. The castle is positioned on top of a mound in a gap in these hills and sits beside the highway forming an impressive defensive position. There is no castle in England more imposing. It is commonly accepted that the castle was built to guard the passage of the hills but it is difficult to understand precisely what it was supposed to have guarded or what danger caused it to be built. The other theory is that a Norman castle-builder may have thought to himself what an excellent site for a castle to control this part of England. Nobody knows precisely when it was built but it is thought to have been during the late 11th century, during the reign of William the Conqueror. It was later improved by his son King Henry I, to make it the most impressive castle in England. The first siege was in the reign of King Stephen, and in the reign of King John it was used as a royal castle to guard his treasure and as a prison. It was also under siege during the Civil War for a total of three years. It was owned by Sir John Bankes who was a supporter of King Charles I. The castle was taken by the Parliamentarians in February 1646 and immediately parliament ruled that it should be demolished. This was implemented and the current state of the ruin is close to how it was left after the demolition.

The Swanage Railway

The ultimate aim of the Southern Steam Trust, which controls the Swanage Railway, is to restore the broken rail link between Swanage and Wareham and to restart a regular daily train service to connect with the rest of the national rail network. This has already successfully been done elsewhere by the Mid-Hants Railway, who operate trains for a considerable length of track between Alresford and Alton. The railway was originally operated by the London & South Western Railway Co and was opened in 1885, after many abortive attempts to get a bill through parliament for a railway to connect to the existing line at Wareham. These attempts failed due to objections about the line going through the centre of Wareham. Finally, in 1880 a local businessman — George Burt — succeeded in getting permission from parliament for a route that avoided Wareham town centre. The line was constructed in just two years and the first train left Swanage station on 20 May 1885. British Rail closed the line and removed the track in 1972, but enthusiasts banded together to reinstate the line and in 1975 the Swanage Railway Society obtained a licence to occupy the Swanage station site. Work has continued to the present day and now the company operates six miles of track between Swanage and Norden, calling at Harman's Cross and Corfe Castle. Trains operate at most times of the year. For further information see the current *Information and Live Steam Programme Leaflet* or telephone 01929 425800. The railway operates a website at www.swanrail.demon.co.uk/.

Starting Point: This ride starts at the Shell Bay Car Park close to the Shell Bay/Sandbanks ferry.

Parking and Toilets: Park in the Shell Bay Car Park. This is a National Trust car park and you may have to pay a small charge if you are not a member. It is also possible to park alongside the road that runs to the ferry without charge — there seems to be plenty of room for parking. Parking is also possible in the car park at Corfe Castle.

Distance: 16.4 miles.

Maps: Ordnance Survey Landranger Sheet 195.

Hills: The outward section of the ride across the bridleways of the heath is very flat. Unfortunately, the return leg from Corfe to Studland cannot claim to be the same. It is like a big dipper fairground ride with more climbs and descents than you can count. You will need to be fit and any children undertaking it will need to be determined and not too young.

Nature of Route: This ride can be conveniently divided into three sections. The first part is off-road and takes place over some delightful shingly bridleways that meander around Studland Heath. On the whole these bridleways provide a good surface for cycling

and there is even a 1¼-mile section of bridleway that is surfaced with tarmac — no doubt funded by the oil extraction activities in the area. The second section is a very quiet, narrow lane that runs below the summit of Brenscombe Hill and Nine Barrow Down. This is a very undulating lane but there are glorious views to be had to the south, with the Swanage Railway running in the valley below. Finally, you return on the B3351 and unclassified roads back to Shell Bay Car Park.

Above:
The Swanage Railway.
Dorset Tourism at Dorset County Council

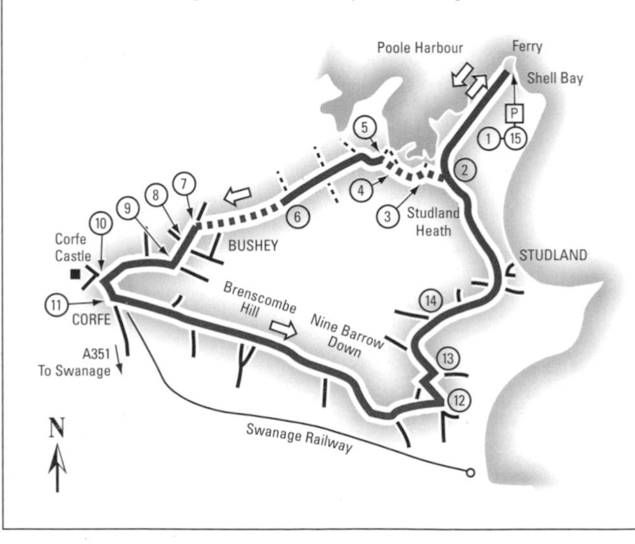

Safety: There is just one busy section of road where care should be taken. This is the A351 through Corfe and although only a short stretch, it is a nasty, fast and twisting piece of road.

Refreshments: There are

not many opportunities for refreshment at country pubs or tea rooms immediately alongside the route. Nearby though, is the village of Corfe with the Bankes Arms Hotel and several other establishments. In Ulwell there is the Village Inn — this is associated with Ulwell Cottage Holiday Park. Also, in Studland there is a good selection of tea rooms and pubs.

Nearest Tourist Information Centre: The White House, Shore Road, Swanage, Dorset BH19 1LB (tel: 01929 422885).

Cycle Hire: Quality Cycle Hire, High Street, Swanage, Dorset (tel: 01929 425050).

Route Instructions:

1. (0.0 miles): Leave the Shell Bay Car Park and cycle away from the ferry to Studland Heath along the flat ferry approach road.

2. (1.5 miles): Turn right on to the bridleway that is marked 'Bridleway to Rempstone Forest'.

3. (2.0 miles): Swing left to avoid the track to Greenland Farm.

4. (2.5 miles): Swing left away from Goathorn Farm continuing on the bridleway to Rempstone Forest.

5. (2.6 miles): You will meet a sealed road. Turn left on to this to continue as directed, 'Bridleway to Rempstone Forest'. Continue on the sealed surface ignoring the possible turning right to 'Ower 3/4' and continue as signposted 'Bushey 2 1/4'.

6. (3.9 miles): At the stop sign (rather unusual for a crossing of bridleways), continue straight on as signposted 'bridleway to Bushey', leaving the sealed surface to join a shingly and sandy bridleway of variable quality.

7. (5.0 miles): The bridleway eventually meets a sealed road (no signpost) at a point under parallel power lines. Turn left here.

8. (5.3 miles): You will join a road on its corner; carry straight on here.

9. (5.6 miles): At the junction with the B3351, turn right as directed 'Corfe Castle 1, Wareham 5'. Take care as this is a much faster moving and busier road than you have travelled on previously during this ride.

10. (6.5 miles): Just after passing under the railway viaduct, at the foot of Corfe Castle, turn left on to the A351 towards the village of Corfe. Although the route is only on this road for a very short time, this is a very busy and unpleasant road so take great care.

11. (6.7 miles): Just before entering Corfe village, turn off left by Brook Cottage under a railway bridge into Sandy Hill Lane. You will continue on this lane without further need for direction for about 5 miles.

12. (11.3 miles): At the give-way junction (there should be a mini-roundabout a couple of hundred yards away if you look right) turn left.

13. (11.7 miles): In Ulwell, turn left on to a busier road.

14. (12.8 miles): At the junction with the B3351, turn right — signposted to Studland. This road takes you through the village of Studland and back to your starting point at Shell Bay Car Park.

15. (16.4 miles): Arrive back at the Shell Bay Car Park.

Above:
Orchids on Studland Heath.

THE OX DROVE WAY

(An elevated ride along the Ox Drove Way with a return along the Ebble Valley)

The green gully at last opens upon the south slope of the hill, upon a wide solitude where runs that old Celtic road called the 'Ox Drove' or 'Ridgeway'. This venerable track, which long preceded any Roman road, runs for many a breezy mile across the county.
Sir Frederick Treves writing in 1906 about the Ox Drove Way in his *Highways and Byways in Dorset*

The Ox Drove Way is a ridgeway that runs for 14¼ miles from a point on the A354 about 6 miles southwest of Salisbury, to Win Green. It is a track for most of its length but in some places stretches of it have been adopted and surfaced to become part of the regularly used road system. Although the track itself is not, strictly speaking, within Hampshire or Dorset, the ride starts from Sixpenny Handley, and thus the start point is just within Dorset. There are many ridgeway tracks running across the chalk hills in the southern counties of England. Many of them have been used since pre-Roman times and this one, no doubt, was mainly a route for cattle or sheep in their passage from one settlement to another. It keeps to the hilltop and to the bare ridge, as at that time the valleys were not cleared and were overgrown with the wildwood. These ridgeways are not prescribed cycle routes. They can be classified as bridleways, byways or roads used as public paths, and depending on their use their surface can provide demanding cycling. At most times of the year though, they are dry due to the chalk subsoil, but increasingly they are being damaged by overuse by four-wheel drive vehicles and, to a lesser extent, horses and motorcycles. Depending on the time of year and the wetness of the season, you may find the Ox Drove Way muddy and flooded, so unless you are a keen off-road enthusiast and like getting soaked and plastered in mud, it would be best to undertake the ride after a period of dry weather. After the initial 4 miles or so on the Ox Drove, we follow the clear waters of the River Ebble for several miles, passing through a number of villages, picturesquely set in the downs. You realise that some of them seem to have changed little in the past hundred years, especially when you cycle through Berwick St John and see the blacksmith busy at his work, with fire burning, hammer working and sparks

Below:
The Ox Drove Way leads off into the distance.

flying. The River Ebble is one of the five chalk streams that flow into Salisbury looking, on the map, like the fingers of a hand. At Broad Chalke we leave the river to climb back on to the downs. One thing that you can almost guarantee is that while you are on the Ox Drove, you will hardly meet a fellow cyclist or walker all day and you will have it to yourself. You will be free to enjoy the skylarks singing overhead, the buzzards flying above the combes, and the yellowhammers singing about their 'little piece of bread and no cheese'.

BACKGROUND AND PLACES OF INTEREST

Sixpenny Handley and its name

Another example of the prevalence of charming and interesting place names in Dorset. However, the reason behind the name is not as interesting as it implies. Despite the fact that from time to time signposts appear with 'To 6d Handley', the place name has nothing to do with money. It has simply arisen from two medieval place names: 'Saxpena' meaning Saxon hilltop and 'Hanlege' meaning high clearing. Sixpenny Handley does have some notoriety, however, as it was at one time the home of Isaac Gulliver, a famous smuggler who was known as 'the gentle smuggler' who never killed a man and who traded in the very innocent commodities (in these days) of gin, silk, lace and tea. It was marriage that brought him to Sixpenny Handley when he married Betty Beale, the daughter of the innkeeper of the Blacksmith's Arms at Thorney Down on the main Salisbury to Blandford road a couple of miles from the village. He eventually took over the inn and started to bring up his family there before moving to the White Hart in Longham and then a newly built lodge at West Howe, Kinson, near Bournemouth in 1780. What made Gulliver different from other Dorset smugglers was that he invested the money gained from his smuggling activities into property that was also often used for more smuggling activities. He eventually took the opportunity of obtaining a pardon for his spirits and tea smuggling activities by a royal proclamation in 1782. He then gave up smuggling spirits and tea, to concentrate on the wine trade and had many storage places along the Dorset coast. He died an extremely wealthy man in 1822.

Cranborne Chase

Only a couple of miles from Sixpenny Handley is Cranborne Chase. A 'chase' was an area of unenclosed forest land used for hunting. At one time this covered a huge area and held 12,000 head of deer, but the forested land has now shrunk to a small area to the south of the Ox Drove on the Wiltshire/Dorset border. It was a lawless place where gentlemen of the district formed themselves into groups of deer hunters. These were aristocratic poachers who often clashed with the rangers and also with the humbler poachers who were poaching, no doubt, because of need. It later became a resort for smugglers and other undesirables and had to be brought under control. It was finally disafforested in 1830, but still remains a very beautiful area.

Starting Point: This ride starts from the Garston Wood Car Park which is about 2 miles north of Sixpenny Handley on the Bowerchalke road.

Parking and Toilets: Park in the car park for the Garston Wood RSPB nature reserve.

Distance: 18.1 miles.

Map: Ordnance Survey Landranger Sheet 184.

Hills: This is a ride of two levels. One level is on the Ox Drove Way on the ridge of the downs at approximately 230m. The other is in the Ebble Valley at a mean height of 100m. There is therefore a stiff climb on the return to the ridge of the downs, which is very steep just after you pass through Bowerchalke.

Nature of Route: The first mile is spent climbing to gain access to the Ox Drove Way, and then about 4 miles is spent actually on the Way. The unsurfaced sections can be heavy going and after rain can be difficult to pass without getting your feet thoroughly wet. The rest of the ride is on quiet country lanes along the Ebble Valley and then back to the top of the downs and downhill to the start point.

Safety: There are no particular hazards associated with this ride.

Refreshments: In Sixpenny Handley (not directly on the route but only 2 miles from the start and end of the ride) there is the Roebuck Inn. In Berwick St John (6 miles), there is the Talbot Inn and at Alvediston (7 miles) is the

Crown Inn — a 17th century free house (just by the turning for Ansty and Tisbury). There is the Three Horseshoes in Ebbesbourne Wake (9 miles); visiting here will necessitate turning right at Route Instruction 8. Finally, there is the Queens Head in Broad Chalke (13 miles)

Nearest Tourist Information Centre: Marsh and Ham Car Park, West Street, Blandford Forum, Dorset DT11 7HD (tel: 01258 454770).

Cycle Hire: Jack Hearne, Salisbury Street, Blandford Forum, Dorset (tel: 01258 452532).

Route Instructions:

1. (0.0 miles): Leave the Garston Wood Car Park and turn left towards Bowerchalke to climb steadily uphill.

2. (1.1 miles): Turn sharp left as signposted to Ebbesbourne Wake and Shaftesbury. This part of the Ox Drove Way is surfaced and runs absolutely straight as far as the eye can see.

3. (2.2 miles): Avoid the sharp right turn on the hairpin bend and continue straight on to join the unsurfaced Ox Drove Way.

4. (4.8 miles): Leave the unsurfaced Ox Drove Way, to join a surfaced road continuing in the same direction.

Above:
The Talbot Inn at Berwick St John.

5. (5.1 miles): Turn right as directed to Berwick St John and cycle down a very steep hill to the village.

6. (5.9 miles): Close to the speed restriction sign, there is a fork — you will need to bear right here.

7. (6.3 miles): Turn right in Berwick St John, just after the forge, and head east towards Broad Chalke.

8. (9.1 miles): At the west end of Ebbesbourne Wake, turn left up the hill if you wish to follow a little bypass that enables you to miss the village. Turn right if you wish to visit the village and the Three Horseshoes pub.

9. (10.0 miles): At the end of the little bypass around the village, turn left in a direction away from the village.

10. (13.0 miles): In Broad Chalke, turn right opposite the Queens Head on the road signposted to Bowerchalke. By the church the road swings sharp right and is signposted 'Bowerchalke 3'.

11. (16.9 miles): Having passed through Bowerchalke toward Sixpenny Handley and overcome the subsequent steep climb back on to the downs, you will come to the junction with the Ox Drove Way (previous Route Instruction 2). Go straight on here to return to the starting point.

12. (18.1 miles): Arrive back at Garston Wood Car Park.

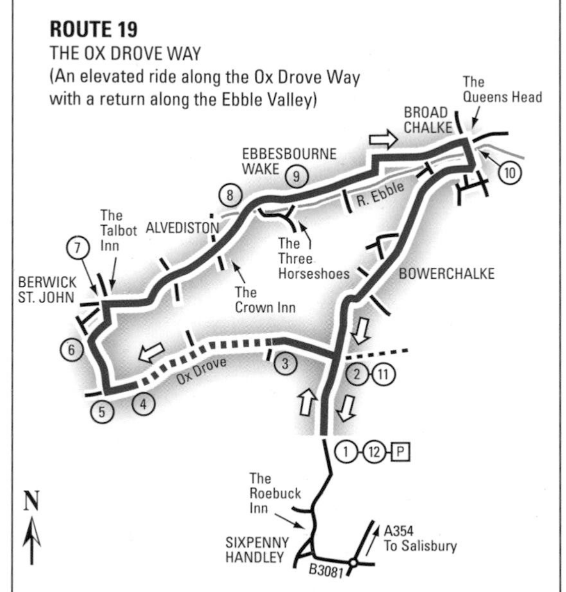

Above:
The Quay at Wareham.

THE PURBECK CYCLEWAY

(A circular ride from Wareham via the rivers Piddle and Frome)

A romantic and unforgettable old town, it lives within its earthen walls, with ramparts north, east, and west, and a river on the south. Is any English town so snugly set as this small place, with its delightful streets, its lovely lanes, its charming houses, its venerable churches, and the green meadows stretching far away?
A description of Wareham from *Arthur Mee's The King's England — Dorset*, first published in 1939

As the title implies, this ride follows the Purbeck Cycleway and you will see the familiar brown signs with a green or blue disk from time to time. However, they will not be of much help to you as waymarking on the route is clockwise, whereas this route takes you anti-clockwise. The reason for riding anti-clockwise is to save the best part of the ride — the crossing of the River Frome and the ride through the Frome Valley — to the end. The first part of the ride, through Wareham Forest, is not the most enjoyable cycling in the world. I suppose it is because everything seems to be straight. Once you are clear of pretty Wareham, for 5 miles the road is straight, almost without exception, and we can probably blame the Romans for this. If this were not bad enough, the part of Wareham Forest that lines the road seems to consist almost entirely of conifers, all standing like soldiers in a line practising their drill. Thankfully, after this, once we get closer to the River Piddle (also known as the Trent), the route quickly improves and we cycle some very pleasant lanes before we cross the river. After the crossing, as you get close to Bovington, you will probably see some real soldiers, rather than trees, practising their drill. Also, if you take a short detour from here you can visit Clouds Hill that was owned by Lawrence of Arabia — see below. The highlight of the ride is the gravel track through the rhododendron-lined conifer forest known as Moreton Drive that leads to the wide, shallow crossing of the River Frome. You can cross by the ford, or the narrow bridge if you dismount. Here there is a good chance you will spot a kingfisher or two. The final part of the ride follows the line of the Frome Valley as you return to Stoborough and then on to Wareham.

BACKGROUND AND PLACES OF INTEREST

Wareham

The town is one of the earliest settlements in Dorset. Situated on an elevated strip of land between the River Frome to the south and the Piddle (or Trent) to the north, and with Poole

Harbour to the east, it made an ideal site for a fortified town. Today it is still surrounded on three sides by earth ramparts, with the River Frome on the fourth side. Originally, Wareham was probably a riverside stronghold built by the Bronze Age Celts, then when the Romans came they strengthened the position and gave it many of its features, such as the four streets that follow the lines of the compass. Wareham is both a romantic and memorable old town. Its streets and walls are steeped in history. Many of the memories are founded upon misfortune, as Wareham has had more than its fair share of disasters. There is probably no place in England that has been under siege so often, or has been burnt so often or reduced to ruins so often. The Danes were very active in the area and took it from the Saxons in 876 and for the following 150 years it was the scene of endless skirmishes, battle and murder. Sometimes it was held by the Danes and then by the Saxons. During the Civil War, the town was nominally held by the Royalists but was laid siege by Parliament, and was raided as something of an entertainment at the weekends. By 1646, Parliament held the town and voted for it to be 'slighted' or reduced to the ground. Fortunately, this was never carried out and the walls of Wareham remain. After a 100 years of peace, it was time for another calamity as Wareham decided to burn itself down in its own great fire.

Clouds Hill

Turn left instead of joining the unsealed track at Route Instruction 12, and this will bring you to Clouds Hill — Lawrence of Arabia's Cottage. T. E. Lawrence, more popularly known as Lawrence of Arabia, was without doubt one of the great Englishmen of the 20th century. He was an excellent scholar and but for the war would probably have become a prominent archaeologist of Syria, Arabia and Palestine. His progress from the Intelligence Department of the Near Eastern Forces to leader and master of the untamed Arab tribes and his ability to unite the Arab peoples were truly remarkable. An equally remarkable facet of his life was that when his work with the Arab peoples was done, he became plain Aircraftsman Shaw and set aside any honours or rewards. His philosophy was that he had performed his appointed task, and there was no reason for any further fuss. He merely wished to live out his life in this peaceful little Dorset cottage. From here, he was in the habit of riding his motorcycle at speed around the nearby lanes. One day he collided with a boy cyclist and after five days died from his injuries at the age of 47. Clouds Hill is in the keeping of the National Trust and stands isolated in heathland amidst the glory of rhododendrons in their season. Here, Aircraftsman T. E. Shaw of the RAF lived very simply with his secretary, with little more than a couch, a table to work at and an armchair. Clouds Hill is open daily from noon, from April to October (tel: 01929 405616 for more information).

Bovington Tank Museum

The museum is an extensive indoor collection of over 300 fighting vehicles that traces the evolution of the tank from the first examples in World War 1 right through to the present day. There are armoured vehicle rides, and various exhibitions including 'The Trench — Tanks on the Somme 1916'. (Tel: 01929 405096 for more information, or visit www.tankmuseum.co.uk.)

Starting Point: This ride starts from the Connigar Lane long-stay car park in Wareham.

Parking and Toilets: Wareham has three types of car park — short-, medium- and long-stay. Only long-stay ones allow you to stay for four hours so it is probably best to use one of these. There are two — Streche Road on the west side of Wareham and Connigar Lane on the east side. I used the Connigar Lane Car Park which is conveniently situated for the quay where there are pubs and toilets, and the town is close by. It is also possible to park at Cold Harbour in Wareham Forest at the beginning of the ride and also opposite the station at Wool — there are public toilets here as well.

Travel by Rail: It is perfectly feasible to travel to the start of this ride by train. Wareham is on the main Waterloo to Weymouth line. For details of the carriage of cycles on this line, please refer to the 'Transporting Cycles' chapter.

Distance: 22.7 miles.

Maps: Ordnance Survey Landranger Sheets 194 and 195.

Hills: Two minor river valleys feature in this ride. The first — the River Piddle — is crossed and consequently there is a fairly stiff climb south from river level at Briantspuddle. After that the ride more or less follows the valley of the River Frome and is therefore generally flat.

Nature of Route: The first part of the ride takes place on very straight unclassified roads through the significantly coniferous Wareham Forest and is not particularly inspiring. This is followed by a much better section involving crossing of the River Piddle (using a footbridge alongside the ford), then some further forest cycling that includes a very pleasant off-road section leading to a further footbridge crossing — this time of the River Frome. The final part of the ride follows the line of the valley of the River Frome as it winds its way to Wareham.

Safety: There are no specific safety hazards associated with this ride.

Refreshments: There is plenty of choice of tea rooms and pubs in Wareham. Around the ride, there is the Silent Woman at Cold Harbour at just over 2 miles. At East Burton there is the Seven Stars at 15 miles, and at Wool there is the Ship Inn, not far from the route at 16 miles. Finally, in Stoborough there is the Kings Arms.

Nearest Tourist Information Centre: Purbeck Information and Heritage Centre, South Street, Wareham (tel: 01929 552740).

Cycle Hire: Trax MTB Hire, Sandford Holiday Park, Wareham (tel: 01202 383898). Bike About, 71 High Street, Swanage (tel: 01929 425050).

Route Instructions:

1. (0.0 miles): Leave the Connigar Lane Car Park using Church Lane, turn right into Church Street, straight over the small give-way road junction to pass the supermarket on the left and then turn left into East Street. Turn right at the traffic lights by the Wareham Town Museum into North Street.

2. (0.6 miles): After you cross the bridge over the River Piddle, take the cycleway to pass under the A351 Wareham bypass and to join Northport. Follow this road as far as the railway signalbox and cross the railway line using the pedestrian crossing.

3. (0.9 miles): At the roundabout on the other side of the crossing, take the Bere road signed as 'Bere Regis 6'.

4. (5.6 miles): Take the left turn marked 'Lane End 1¼, Culeaze, 1½, Wool 6'.

5. (6.8 miles): Turn right as signposted to 'Bere Regis 1½'.

6. (7.5 miles): At the give-way junction you will join a more significant road on its bend (signpost missing at the time of riding). Turn right here and then almost immediately take a left turn as indicated to 'Turners Puddle 1¼'.

7. (8.0 miles): At the next junction take a right turn as signposted to 'Turners Puddle ¾'. This is marked as a no through road for vehicles. The road eventually peters out by the farm, at which point you should turn left

Above:
Information board at Wareham Quay.

through the ford or use the accompanying pedestrian bridge to cross the River Piddle. Follow the unsealed track on the other side to the river until you meet the sealed road.

8. (8.9 miles): At the junction with the sealed road, turn right toward Briantspuddle.

9. (9.7 miles): In Briantspuddle at the give-way junction (opposite house No 12), turn left as signposted to Bovington Camp to face the steep climb out of the village.

10. (10.1 miles): At the crossroads, proceed straight on as signposted to Bovington.

11. (10.8 miles): At the give-way junction, just after passing under the high voltage power lines, (signpost broken at the time of riding) turn right along a road through Moreton Forest that is completely straight to the next instruction.

12. (11.1 miles): At the cross-roads you need to go straight on down the unsealed track (unmarked at the time of riding). This is a very pleasant track through the forest. Little direction is necessary except to fork right to avoid a private track just before the river. At the ford, take the long and narrow footbridge to cross the River Frome. Continue on the other side until you come to Moreton.

13. (12.6 miles): In Moreton just after passing the post office, you will meet a sealed road again. Turn left for 'East Burton 2½, Wool 3¾'.

14. (15.9 miles): You will arrive in Wool by the East Burton road at the Texaco garage. Turn right here and then immediately left as signposted for West Lulworth.

15. (16.1 miles). Turn left into Bindon Lane as signposted 'Bindon Abbey ½, West Holme 3¾, East Holme 3¾'.

16. (19.0 miles): At the junction with the B3070 cross straight over and continue on Holme Lane. Do not be concerned about the red flags — these merely mark the edge of the military range.

17. (21.3 miles): At the end of Holme Lane, by the Springfield Country Hotel, turn left as signposted for 'Stoborough 1, Wareham 1¾'.

18. (21.7 miles): At the junction with the A351 Wareham/Swanage road, turn left and immediately right and follow the signs for Stoborough.

19. (21.9 miles): At the give-way junction, by the village pump in Stoborough, turn left as signposted to the village centre, and you will soon see Wareham ahead.

20. (22.4 miles): You will find yourself back at the main traffic lights in Wareham. Turn right to retrace your outward route back to the Connigar Lane Car Park.

21. (22.7 miles): Arrive back at the car park.

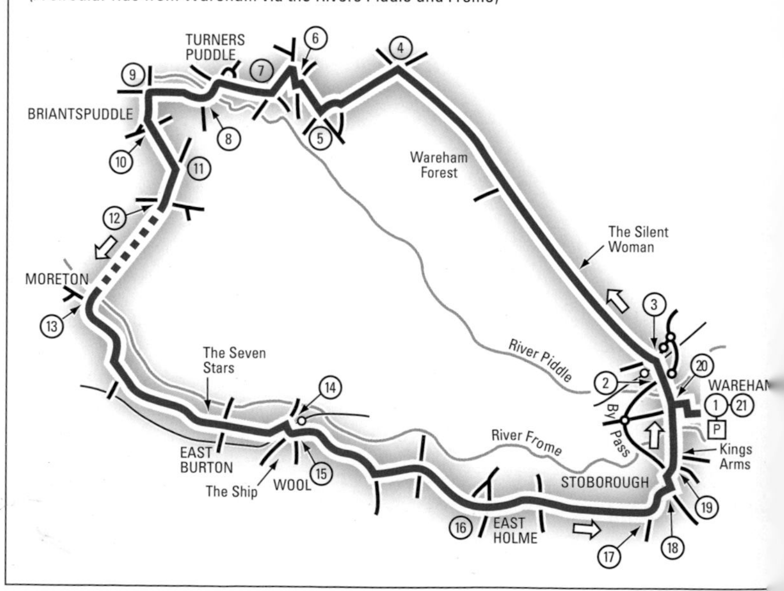

BLANDFORD FORUM AND THE TARRANTS

(A circular ride from Blandford Forum through the villages of the Tarrant stream)

The town is seen at its best when viewed from the grey many-arched bridge which crosses the Stour. The river here is a lazy stream, flecked with water-lilies, fringed with rushes, and so overhung with trees that the swallows fluttering over its surface seem to be sporting a green cloister.

Sir Frederick Treves writing in 1906 about Blandford Forum in his *Highways and Byways in Dorset*

When I looked at the map and spotted the quiet-looking 'back' road that runs due north from Blandford to Shaftesbury, I thought to myself that this would be an excellent escape route from the town into the country. Unfortunately, this road turned out to be disappointing as it was much busier than I imagined, so I decided to turn off as soon as possible at the Everley Hill cross-roads, and head for Tarrant Gunville. The cyclist in Dorset cannot fail to become interested in the place names of the county as they are so unusual and unique, and Tarrant Gunville — and for that matter the other Tarrants — are no exception. According to one source, the name Tarrant arises from the name 'Terente' meaning trespasser, presumably from its habit of occasionally flooding the valley and villages

Above:
The ford and bridge at Tarrant Monkton.

along its course. In this ride we visit all eight of the Tarrant villages, from Tarrant Gunville at the source of the stream down to Tarrant Crawford where it loses its identity and enters the River Stour. It is a leisurely ride often accompanied closely by the gurgling waters. I cycled the route on an extremely hot and dusty day in June and my main memory of the ride is of cattle drinking at the water's edge and a group of young teenagers keeping cool in the water at Tarrant Rushton. Like all chalk streams, the Tarrant looks so crystal clear and pure and inviting on a hot day.

BACKGROUND AND PLACES OF INTEREST

Blandford Forum

This small market town nestles on the banks of the River Stour, on the edge of Blackmoor Vale. It has experienced a series of fires that began in 1579 when the town was nearly destroyed, further fires in 1677 and 1713, and then the Great Fire in 1731, which destroyed all but 40 houses. Fortunately, architects and builders John and William Bastard, pupils of Sir Christopher Wren, were able to bring their skill and inspiration into rebuilding the town. It is now one of the best preserved Georgian town centres in the south of England. The Market Place is a conservation area having six Grade 1 listed buildings. The Great Fire was also responsible for stamping out an epidemic of smallpox that was raging at the time. The sick had to be carried out of the town and laid in fields, under the bridge and along hedges. It was amazing that only one person died. Blandford Forum was once famous for its point lace, which was said to be the finest in the whole of England and valued at £30 a yard. The Milldown is a conservation project that was set up in 1990 in an area on the northwestern edge of Blandford. It is an area of woodland, grassland and scrub with a wide variety of trees and plants that support a rich insect and wildlife population. Visitors can enjoy the area by walking or having picnics and there is a safe fenced play area for children. More information about the project can be obtained by reading the information boards or by joining one of the guided walks (tel: 01258 472441/471130 for more information).

Tarrant Gunville

Just south of the village, on the left-hand side, you will not fail to notice the parklands and lodge house of Eastbury House. This was built by George Bubb, the son of an apothecary from Weymouth. When 29, he inherited a fortune from his uncle George Dodington and became a man of ambition and changed his name to George Bubb Dodington. He spent some time in politics and was raised to the peerage as Baron Melcombe. The house was built between 1718 and 1738 at an enormous cost and was reputedly one of the grandest in the kingdom at the time. Lord Melcombe reputedly slept in a bed surrounded by peacock feathers. He died while still young and most of the house, with the exception of the one remaining wing, was demolished as it could not be maintained. The church has a memorial to Thomas Wedgwood, who was son of the more famous Josiah. He was an early experimenter in photography and eventually built a basic camera, but his contribution to the science of photography was limited because he was unable to discover a technique for permanently fixing his images. He died in 1805, at the age of only 34, with his work incomplete, but he was the founder of photography on the principle of making pictures by the action of light.

Above:
An example of a Dorset signpost with its grid reference.

Royal Signals Museum

This nearby museum tells the story of the men and women of the Royal Corps of Signals from the Crimean War to the Falklands, the Gulf War and up to the present day. A series of interactive displays and exhibitions inform visitors about battlefield communications. There are many hands-on working exhibits. The museum also depicts the stories of the Special Operations Executive (SOE), the ATS, the Long Range Desert Group and SAS Signals. Visitors need to take some form of identification (tel: 01258 482248 for more information).

Cavalcade of Costume

The Cavalcade of Costume in Blandford Forum is displayed in Lime Tree House, near the famous Georgian market place. This unique collection has been gathered over 35 years and amounts to over 500 items dating from the 1730s right up to the 1950s. Mrs Betty Penny was awarded the MBE in 1984 for her amazing achievement and for raising almost £500,000 for charity by travelling around the country showing her remarkable collection. The garments and their array of accessories are now on permanent display, providing a family visit that is both educational and fun. There is also a tea room, shop and garden (tel: 01258 453006 for more information).

Starting Point: This ride starts from the Langton Road Car Park in Blandford Forum (see below).

Parking and Toilets: Park in Blandford Forum at the Langton Road Car Park long-term section — located close to the Kwik-Save supermarket. This car park is on the south side of the town, close to the river. Public toilets are provided.

Distance: 16.9 miles.

Maps: Ordnance Survey Landranger Sheets 194 and 195.

Hills: There are very few hills on this ride as for the most part it follows the course of the Tarrant Stream.

Nature of Route: Having left the Blandford Forum built-up area, this ride follows unclassified surfaced country roads throughout almost all of its length. Unfortunately, the initial road that is used to leave the town and for the first four miles of the ride can be rather busy. Care should be taken on this section and my advice would be that it should only be ridden by a competent cyclist and not by very young children. The majority of the ride follows the line and level of the Tarrant and is therefore very easy going without any hills and is also relatively traffic-free. The final leg back into the town is also very quiet.

Safety: Care should be taken on the initial stretch as far as the Everley Hill cross-roads and also when crossing the A354 and B3082.

Refreshments: Unfortunately, this ride has suffered from the modern phenomena of the disappearance of country pubs, and it is not now possible to stop at the pub in Tarrant Gunville, as you once could. However, at Tarrant Monkton, there is the Langton Arms (where you will need to turn right to cross the river at 9.4 miles), and there is also the True Lovers Knot at Tarrant Keyneston. Obviously there are plenty of refreshment opportunities in Blandford Forum.

Nearest Tourist Information Centre: Marsh and Ham Car Park, West Street, Blandford Forum, Dorset DT11 7HD (tel: 01258 454770).

Cycle Hire: Jack Hearne, Salisbury Street, Blandford Forum, Dorset (tel: 01258 452532).

Route Instructions:

1. (0.0 miles): Leave Langton Road Car Park in Blandford Forum by turning right and then immediately left into St Leonards Avenue, and then left into Queens Road.

2. (0.6 miles): At the end of Queens Road, turn right into Salisbury Road.

3. (0.9 miles): When you are close to the church turn left into Higher Shaftesbury Road.

4. (1.5 miles): At the end of Higher Shaftesbury Road you will come to a roundabout. Go straight on here as directed to Melbury Abbas.

5. (4.0 miles): Turn right at the Everley Hill cross-roads (GR 889120) as signposted to Tarrant Gunville.

6. (6.3 miles): At the three-way junction turn left to Tarrant Gunville.

7. (6.5 miles): In Tarrant Gunville (GR 926127), turn right as directed to 'Tarrant Hinton 1½, Blandford Forum 6, Salisbury 19'.

8. (8.0 miles): At the staggered cross-roads, turn right on to the main road (A354) and then immediately left on to the road signposted 'Tarrant Launceston 1 mile, Tarrant Monkton 1½ miles'.

9. (13.0 miles): In Tarrant Keyneston, at the junction with the B3082 by the True Lovers Knot pub, go straight on as directed to 'T. Crawford 1¾, Spettisbury 3'.

10. (14.2 miles): At the Keyneston Mill Corner junction, turn right as directed to 'Blandford 2¼ miles'.

11. (16.5 miles): At the junction with the A354, use the underpass to go under this busy road, by swinging left down to the river and passing under the bridge to join the lane.

12. (16.9 miles): Arrive back at the Langton Road Car Park.

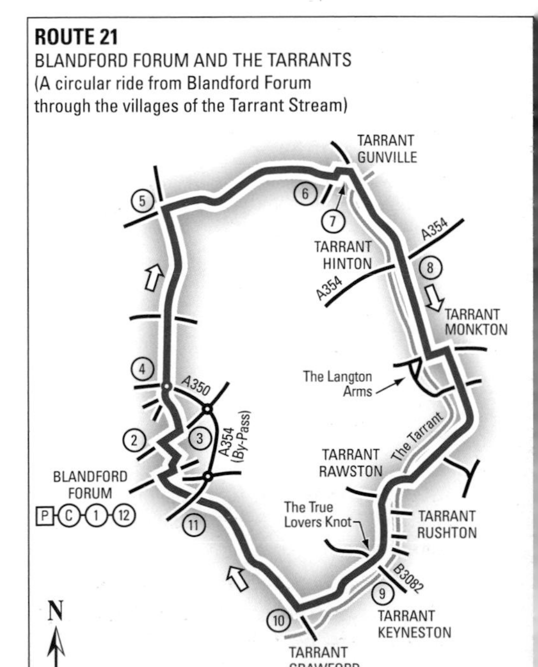

SHAFTESBURY TO CHILD OKEFORD

(A circular ride from Dorset's hilltop town)

There will be found, on the other hand, dignified old houses with stone mullioned windows, moss-covered walls crowned by apple blossom, lanes with brown-thatched cottages where a path of cobble stones leads through a garden to a porch of honeysuckle.
Sir Frederick Treves writing about Shaftesbury in his *Highways and Byways in Dorset*

This ride starts and finishes from the Saxon hilltop town of Shaftesbury. For over 20 years I lived in Warminster a few miles to the north of Shaftesbury and although I travelled from that direction to Shaftesbury many times, I was never truly aware of the elevation of the town and of the way that it is perched on the end of a ridge. It is only when you undertake a cycle ride to the south and east and you experience the extremely steep climb to return to town at the end of the ride, that you are made painfully aware of how high this hilltop town is, although if you are a really keen, young and energetic cyclist and not just a potterer like me, then I am sure you will find it manageable. However, it has its compensations as you ride or walk through the town, as a gap between the houses will regularly appear where you will obtain a sudden view of an apparently limitless valley, with a walled lane running toward the valley bottom. This is one of the longer rides in the book and passes through some pleasant villages, accompanied for most of the outward leg of the ride by a fine range of downs on the left marking the escarpment of Cranborne Chase. At the furthest limit of the ride we reach Child Okeford in the shelter of Hambledon Hill and possibly pause for a snack before we return to Shaftesbury, or Shaston as Thomas Hardy and the locals like to know it.

BACKGROUND AND PLACES OF INTEREST

Shaftesbury

It is the height of Shaftesbury at 229m above sea level that has been the dominant factor in its history. The present town was founded by King Alfred in AD880, after his defeat of the Vikings, because of its strategic importance overlooking the surrounding land. He was confident enough of its invulnerability that he founded an abbey for his daughter here. The abbey was a centre for pilgrimage in medieval times due to the burial there of King Edward the Martyr. It survived the centuries until the dissolution of the monasteries by Henry VIII. As you stroll through the town, you will frequently catch a view between the houses of the Blackmoor Vale to the south and west. Often you will see a lane that descends from the hilltop and the most well known of these is Gold Hill, that several years ago was made famous in the Hovis bread advertisement. It is a cobbled lane that at the top has the attractive old town hall and the old church of St Peter. And as you climb, at your side are thatched and tiled cottages that are seemingly placed on steps to keep a strong foothold. In addition to the excavated remains of the abbey (open in the summer months with its museum, garden and audio tours), there is the 17th century Ox House referred to in Thomas Hardy's *Jude the Obscure*, and the Tudor-style town hall and Grosvenor Hotel — a 400-year-old coaching inn.

Old Wardour Castle

This unusual hexagonal castle is perfectly set among acres of woodland and a nearby lake. This peaceful setting masks a violent

Left:
Enjoying the sunshine near Hambledon Hill.

Above:
Some of the stalest bread in Dorset.

siege in the Civil War when Blanche, second wife of Baron Arundell of Wardour, defended the castle in 1643 against a force of rebels. Although having only 50 men to support her, of whom only half were soldiers, and with women loading muskets, she defended the castle against 1,300 men for five days. Eventually she surrendered on honourable terms, but the rebels violated the agreement and plundered the castle and park. The ruins that remain are relatively complete and with the tall windows are a good example of late 14th and early 15th century castle design. In recent times the castle was used as a location for the film *Robin Hood, Prince of Thieves*. The castle is open daily from April to November and during the winter months from Wednesday to Sunday (tel: 01747 870487 for further information).

Chettle House
About 9 miles southeast of Shaftesbury lies the manor house of the village of Chettle. This fine example of a small country house is built in the English baroque style. The gardens are especially worthy of note and contain many chalk-loving varieties that would interest the enthusiast. The house is open daily during the summer months. For further information on opening times contact Shaftesbury Tourist Information Centre (see below).

Starting Point: This ride starts from Coppice Street Car Park — see below.

Parking and Toilets: If starting the ride from Shaftesbury, park in Coppice Street Car Park. This is a free long-term car park and there are public toilets here. The car park is at the bottom end of the High Street — take the turning by the post office.

Distance: 17.6 miles.

Maps: Ordnance Survey Landranger Sheets 183 and 194.

Hills: The descent and subsequent ascent between Shaftesbury and the surrounding vale is very steep and would be too much for young children or for those who are not fit. Otherwise the rest of the ride is undulating but has no hills of significance.

Nature of Route: This ride follows quiet country lanes, with short distances on B roads.

Safety: There are no particular hazards associated with this ride.

Refreshments: Plenty of cafés and pubs in Shaftesbury. There are two pubs in Child Okeford — the Baker's Arms and the Saxon Inn (careful that you don't miss this one as it is set back behind a yellow-painted house). Nearby, at Okeford Fitzpaine, there is the Royal Oak.

Nearest Tourist Information Centre: Shaftesbury Tourist Information Centre, 8 Bell Street, Shaftesbury, Dorset SP7 8AE (tel: 01747 853514).

Cycle Hire: Dorset Cycle Hire, Stalbridge (tel: 01963 362476). Stalbridge is about 12 miles from Shaftesbury.

Route Instructions:

1. (0.0 miles): From Coppice Street Car Park in Shaftesbury, turn right and proceed down the hill. With the post office on your right, take a right at the give-way junction to cycle up the High Street.

2. (0.2 miles): Turn left at the town hall to find the famous Gold Hill. This is extremely steep and also cobbled for much of the way so that you may wish to walk this bit. At the bottom of Gold Hill, turn right into St James Street and proceed to the end.

3. (0.6 miles): Turn left at the end of St James

Above:
Signpost near Child Okeford.

Street as signposted to Guy's Marsh, Manston and Sturminster Newton. You will experience a steep descent under overhanging hazel trees.

4. (1.2 miles): Bear left as directed to Twyford.

5. (4.0 miles): In the village of Bedchester, travel straight on at the crossroads as directed to Farrington and Child Okeford.

6. (5.3 miles): Turn left at the junction where the signpost was broken at the time of riding. The best way to identify this junction is that the other road (the one that you don't want) is marked 'The Orchards 1¼'.

7. (5.8 miles): At the give-way junction, turn right as directed to 'Child Okeford and Shillingstone' and continue on this road all the way into Child Okeford village.

8. (7.6 miles): In Child Okeford, by the war memorial, turn right — away from the Baker's Arms to leave the village — as directed to Manston and Gillingham.

9. (10.0 miles): At the junction with the B3091, turn right as indicated to 'Shaftesbury 6¼ Gillingham 8¼' miles.

10. (10.6 miles): After passing the village of Manston and the Plough, turn left off the B3091 and as signposted to 'Marnhull East Stour and Gillingham'.

11. (12.1 miles): Turn right at the crossroads in the direction of 'Margaret Marsh 1 mile' towards Shaftesbury on the hilltop ahead of you.

12. (14.0 miles): At the give-way junction with the broken fingerpost, turn left and just before the road swings hard right, turn right.

13. (15.7 miles): Turn left at the junction with the B3091 (this is alongside a rather untidy farm).

14. (16.4 miles): Rejoin your outward route and climb the hill into Shaftesbury. Retrace your route to the Coppice Street Car Park.

15. (17.6 miles): Arrive back at Coppice Street Car Park.

ROUTE 22
SHAFTESBURY TO CHILD OKEFORD
(A circular ride from Dorset's hilltop town)

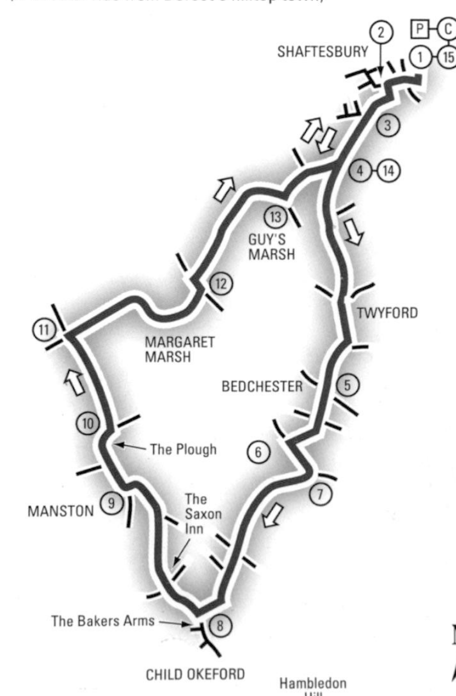

THE WINTERBORNE VILLAGES

(A linear route from Winterborne Kingston to Okeford Hill)

The thatched houses of this quiet village cluster round a noble lime whose fragrance fills the place in due season.
Part of the description of Winterborne Stickland from *Arthur Mee's The King's England — Dorset*, first published in 1939.

This is a very simple ride with hardly any directions being necessary, and yet is one of the best in this book. There are two options. You can either enjoy a very flat and short ride of 11 miles (there and back) to Winterborne Stickland. Alternatively you can continue with a gradual climb of 131m to Okeford Hill picnic spot (the only steep gradient is right at the end between Turnworth and Okeford Hill). If you take the latter option this amounts to an 18-mile ride. When I did the ride it was one of those summer days where there was a thick blanket of cloud that stayed with me throughout the day, so I had no view from Okeford Hill at all, but from looking at the topography of the land on the map, I am sure that there are good views to look forward to. I just hope that you will be luckier than I was with the West Country weather.

BACKGROUND AND PLACES OF INTEREST

Winterbornes and Winterbournes

A winterborne is a stream that usually only runs in the winter months. I say 'usually' as the Winterborne featured here was still running strongly when I did this ride well into July of this very wet early summer of 2000. There is a similar stream in the south of Dorset and one in Wiltshire (spelt Winterbourne). If you avoid the inclusion of Winterburn in your list of Winterbo(u)rne place names, then there are at least 17 occurrences of this name in Britain. In Hampshire and Sussex these winter-rising springs are also known as Lavants. They tend to be a feature of chalk hills and flow as clear, gushing streams, often hidden by wild flowers and weeds, that suddenly dry up, usually in June. I have heard that the older village people can tell almost to the day when the stream will dry up. The settlements on the course of the stream usually have Winterborne names. Eight places on the Blandford Winterborne between its source and where it flows into the River Stour at Sturminster Marshall have Winterborne in the name. On this ride we visit four of the eight.

Milton Abbas

Only a couple of miles away from the route is the picturesque village of Milton Abbas. It is an attractive but odd village of similar houses set on wide strips of lawn laid either side of the main street. It was built in the 1770s by Joseph Damer who was Earl of Dorchester. Next to the old abbey building, he had built himself a magnificent house and came to the opinion that the existing old town was an eyesore. Despite fierce opposition, he demolished all of the existing houses and built the present attractive model village of thatched cob cottages. In the centre of the village are sited some 17th century brick and flint almshouses, and the 18th century church, which was designed in late Georgian style to blend in with the village.

Milton Abbey

This huge gothic mansion is built on the site of an old abbey originally founded in 938 by King Athelstan. Only the old abbot's hall and the abbey church remain of the original foundation. The church houses a superb carved oak shrine, which was used for keeping the consecrated host. It is unique as all others in the country were destroyed during the Reformation.

Milton Park Farm Museum

This fascinating museum is accommodated in a former cart-horse stable roofed with thatch. There is an extensive collection of rural, agricultural and domestic bygones built up by the Fookes family. Outside the stable there is a unique collection of chimney pots and you can select herbs from the herb train. There is a play area for children where they can see bantams, calves, donkeys, ducks, goats, horses, Jacob sheep and pigs.

Starting Point: This ride starts from Church Lane in Winterborne Kingston (see below).

Parking and Toilets: There is no car park in Winterborne Kingston. Lanes in the village are narrow, and in my view the best (and probably only) place that you can park to avoid obstruction is outside the church in Church Lane.

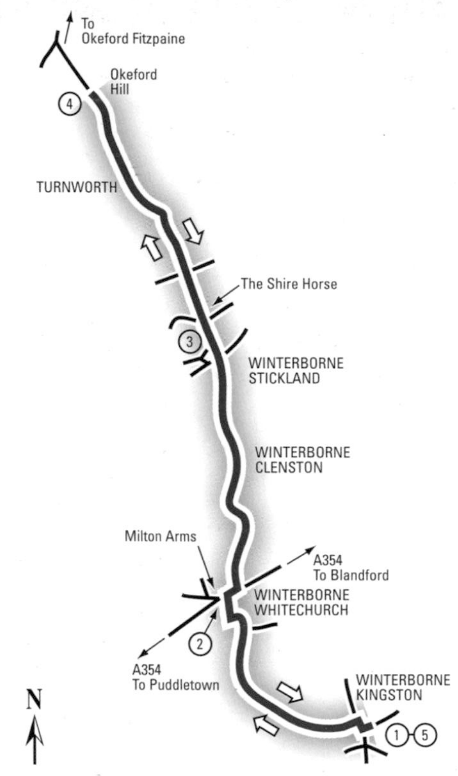

Distance: 11.4 or 18.2 miles.

Map: Ordnance Survey Landranger Sheet 194.

Hills: The first part of this ride as far as Winterborne Stickland has no significant gradient as it follows the course of the Winterborne stream. If you continue the ride to Okeford Hill viewpoint you will experience a steady climb to Turnworth and then a short steep climb to the top.

Nature of Route: This ride is on quiet, unclassified country lanes that follow the course of the Winterborne stream as far as Winterborne Stickland and then leaves it to climb Okeford Hill.

Safety: Be careful as you cross the A354 at Winterborne Whitechurch, as this is a busy road.

Refreshments: The Milton Arms at Winterborne Whitechurch at just under 3 miles. The Shire Horse in Winterborne Stickland at just under 6 miles.

Nearest Tourist Information Centre: Marsh and Ham Car Park, West Street, Blandford Forum, Dorset DT11 7HD (tel: 01258 454770).

Cycle Hire: Jack Hearne, Salisbury Street, Blandford Forum, Dorset (tel: 01258 452532).

Below:
The Shire Horse at Winterborne Stickland.

Route Instructions:

1. (0.0 miles): From Church Lane in Winterbourne Kingston, with the church on your right, cycle to the end of Church Street and turn right on to the main road through the village and then take the next turn left into West Street as signposted to 'Winterborne Whitechurch 2¾, Milton Abbas 5½'.

2. (2.7 miles): At the Milton Arms in Winterborne Whitechurch, turn right on to the A354, and then almost immediately turn left into Whatcombe Lane as signposted 'Winterborne Clenston 1¾', Winterborne Stickland 3'. You should continue on this road without further direction to Winterbourne Stickland.

3. (5.7 miles): In Winterborne Stickland you can either terminate your ride with a picnic on the village green or refreshment at the Shire Horse if you wish. Continue straight on through the village if you are going to Okeford Hill picnic spot.

4. (9.1 miles): Arrive at Okeford Hill picnic spot. Return to your start point by retracing your outward route.

5. (18.2 miles): Arrive back at Winterborne Kingston.

GILLINGHAM TO HINDON USING THE WILTSHIRE CYCLEWAY

(A circular ride following part of the Wiltshire Cycleway and parts of the National Byway and North Dorset Cycleway)

Hindon is a delightful little village, so rustic and pretty amidst its green, swelling downs, with great woods crowning the heights beyond . . .

W. H. Hudson writing in 1910 from *A Shepherd's Life*

This ride shares parts of its course with no less than three cycleways — the Wiltshire Cycleway, the North Dorset Cycleway and the National Byway — and the choice of these lanes by the sponsoring authorities provides strong confirmation that the ride is likely to be relatively traffic-free. The landscape is still almost as delightful as in Hudson's day and the section where you descend into Hindon from East Knoyle is especially so. Unfortunately, hiding behind this beauty is a history of hardship and suffering and confirmation of man's inherent inhumanity to man in these parts, especially in the early 19th century, when agricultural wages were insufficient to support a family without recourse to poaching or stealing; when the farmers 'got rid of' their labourers after every harvest and left them and their families to survive the winter in whatever way they could by gathering dead wood and trying to sell it in the villages, or of course stealing sheep or game for the table. The judges of the time did not distinguish between a man stealing a sheep to survive and a systematic thief who stole to make money. They would therefore sometimes hang a starving man for stealing a sheep (for sheep stealing was a capital offence), or if the judge was disposed to be merciful he would merely order transportation for life! One of the worst examples on record was that of the judge who handed down a sentence of transportation for life for a youth of 18 who stole a pocket-handkerchief. Fortunately, the awful poverty of these Dorset and south Wiltshire villages is now long gone and you can take time to enjoy this beautiful high downland at your leisure.

BACKGROUND AND PLACES OF INTEREST

Gillingham

This is the most northerly town in Dorset and it has a long history, as the existence of the nearby New Stone Age Longbury Barrow will testify. Although the Saxons first established Gillingham it was not until the 1850s that the town saw a significant growth in prosperity. In the Middle Ages it was the seat of a royal hunting lodge. This palace became the 'Sandringham' of the time. Henry I, II and III and King John visited, and Edward I also spent a Christmas here. The nearby royal forest was used for hunting the King's deer but was deforested by Charles I, the palace, after going into decline, having been destroyed by Edward III in 1369. Traces of the rampart and moat can still be seen in a green close called the King's Court, but it is said that the stones from the palace building were taken away and used to mend the roads or build other royal properties in the south of England. The artist John Constable visited Gillingham in the early 1820s and painted several pictures including the old town bridge and Parnham Mill, which now hangs in the Tate Gallery. Although Gillingham grew as a mill town for silk from 1769, it was the arrival of the railway at the end of the 1850s that led to a steady growth as both a commercial and industrial town that has continued to the present day. A museum, adjoining the new county library in Chantry Fields, was built in 1996 and chronicles the history of the town, and copies of Constable's paintings are on show there.

East Knoyle

The main and perhaps only point of interest for the visitor to East Knoyle is that it was the birthplace of Sir Christopher Wren. The rector, a Dr Wren, had two sons called Christopher. The first was 'born, baptised and dead in the same hour' in 1631. It was stated by Dr Wren that the second was born on 20 October 1632, but the baptismal entry in the church records, also made by Dr Wren, gives 26 October 1631. In all, Dr Wren had 11 children. A convinced loyalist, he left Knoyle when the Great Rebellion broke out and went to Windsor. The old rectory was pulled down in 1880.

Hindon

Looking at this little village now it is difficult to imagine the story it has to tell. Once,

Hindon was an important market and session town and a parliamentary borough returning two members. It also had 13 public houses! Before the Reform Bill, the candidates outrageously bribed the people who lived here. It was the order of the day that before an election every householder received 20 guineas from the candidate of his or her choice, and four to six weeks' worth of free beer from any of the 13 pubs. It was even known for some hard-up householders to pledge their 20 guineas to a tradesman before an election! After the Reform Bill Hindon was deprived of its glory and later, when the London & South Western Railway line from Salisbury to Yeovil made its station at Tisbury, it fell into decay, dwindling to the small village it is now. The Lamb Inn, in the centre, is one of the remaining pubs and W. H. Hudson, the countryside writer, stayed here in the spring and summer of 1909 while researching information for *A Shepherd's Life*. In the book he recalls many anecdotes and perhaps the most interesting is of a family called Rawlings, who were tenants of Lower Pertwood Farm, near Hindon. The children in the family had unusual names. Three of the girls were called Faith, Hope and Charity and three of the boys, Justice, Morality and Fortitude.

Above:
Hindon

Farmer Rawlings had a serious disagreement with the local rector over the question of a church bell being tolled at funerals. When three of his family died he refused to bury them and instead kept their coffins in an outhouse for several years. The house was then nicknamed the 'Dead House'. Eventually the dead disappeared and Farmer Rawlings gave up the farm.

Starting Point: This ride starts from the High Street Car Park in Gillingham — see below.

Parking and Toilets: I parked in the High Street Car Park, where there are toilets. There is a long-stay section, where prices are very low. By the time of publication of this book there may be no charge at all as a free parking experiment was underway.

Travel by Rail: It is perfectly feasible to travel to the start of this ride by train. Gillingham is on the Salisbury to Exeter line. For details of carriage of cycles on this line, please refer to the 'Transporting Cycles' chapter.

Distance: 20.5 miles.

Maps: Ordnance Survey Landranger Sheets 183 and 184.

Hills: This ride is in rolling downland country and therefore it is inevitable that there are some hills to climb. However, the only significant one is after you leave Hindon.

Nature of Route: This ride takes place over some very quiet, unclassified country lanes. The first part of the ride shares its course as far as East Knoyle with the Wiltshire Cycleway. This is a route that offers a choice of six circuits of 70 to 160 miles. During the ride you also find signs referring to the North Dorset Cycleway and the National Byway. These also offer long-distance routes on quiet roads and you will find details about these in the 'Cycling Initiatives by Public Bodies' chapter at the end of the book.

Safety: Take care when you cross the A350 at East Knoyle and Semley. This is a very busy and fast road and it is probably best to dismount when negotiating these junctions.

Refreshments: There are several pubs in Gillingham at the start and end of your ride. At 6 miles there is the Seymour Arms in East Knoyle — about 1/2 mile from the route. In Hindon at 8 miles there is the historic Lamb Inn and also the Grosvenor Arms that are immediately on the route.

Nearest Tourist Information Centre: 8 Bell Street, Shaftesbury, Dorset SP7 8AE (tel: 01747 853514).

Cycle Hire: Dorset Cycle Hire, Stalbridge (tel: 01963 362476). Stalbridge is about 11 miles from Gillingham.

Route Instructions:

1. (0.0 miles): From the Gillingham High Street Car Park, turn right into the High Street, swing right into St Martins Square to cycle with the church on your left, and then take the first right into a one-way street known as Queen Street, but is unmarked. At the end of Queen Street, at the give-way junction, turn right into Bay Road as signposted to 'Knoyles and Hindon'.

2. (2.3 miles): At the crossroads, you will join the Wiltshire Cycleway by going straight on, again as directed to 'Knoyles and Hindon'.

3. (4.1 miles): By Park Corner Farm, turn right as signposted 'East Knoyle 2'. You will see Wiltshire Cycleway signs on the signpost, reassuring you that you are on the correct route.

4. (5.6 miles): In Underhill (after climbing a steep hill), turn right down a very narrow lane as directed to East Knoyle — the signpost was very rickety at the time of cycling. You will descend into East Knoyle along some delightful sunken lanes.

5. (6.5 miles): Where Church Road meets the old main road by the war memorial, turn left; you will leave the Wiltshire Cycleway at this point. After a few yards you will meet the new A350 that now bypasses East Knoyle. Be careful as this is a very fast road and it will probably be safer to dismount. Turn left here for a few yards and then cross the road to take the road signposted to 'Hindon'.

6. (8.6 miles): Turn right as directed to 'Hindon Tisbury and Salisbury' to enter Hindon. Take care here as traffic approaches fast from the left.

7. (8.9 miles): In Hindon, take the right turn by the Lamb Inn — there is a signpost to Tisbury hidden away by the telephone box. The route is lined with pollarded trees.

8. (9.0 miles): Turn right opposite School Lane and then almost immediately bear left (avoiding the Dene) to climb the hill. You will experience some testing ascents and descents.

9. (10.8 miles): Turn right as signposted to 'Semley' to descend the steep hill through pleasant coppiced woodland.

10. (12.0 miles): At the little crossroads, cross straight over as directed to 'Semley' and you will pass over a little bridge over a stream.

11. (13.5 miles): At the staggered junction, turn right and immediately left as directed to Station Road Shaftesbury.

12. (14.2 miles): At a further staggered junction (this time with the A350) turn right on to the A350 and immediately left as signposted to 'Motcombe 2½". Again, take care here as traffic moves fast on this road.

13. (16.1 miles): At this junction there are two alternative signposted ways to Gillingham. Take the right turn signposted 'Mere 4 Gillingham 4'. Ignore the left option that is also signposted to Gillingham.

14. (18.2 miles): Turn left at the cross-roads as signposted 'Gillingham 2'.

15. (20.2 miles): On return to Gillingham, by Queen Street Post Office, swing left into Queen Street (unmarked). Take care here as this becomes a one-way street, but there is a cycle path on the pavement that enables you to continue against the flow of traffic.

16. (20.5 miles): Arrive back at the High Street Car Park.

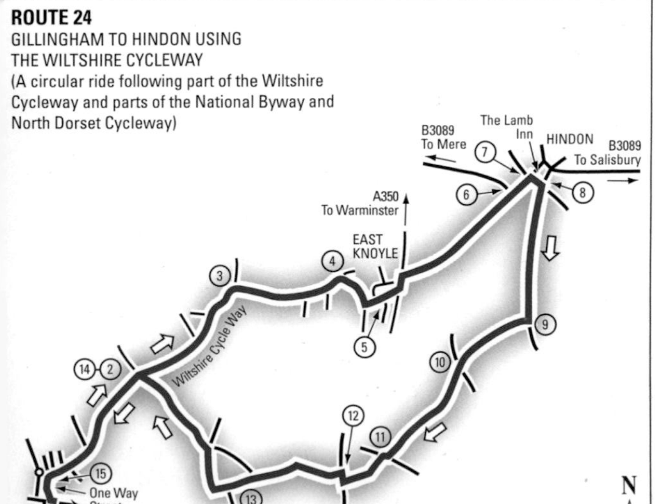

Above:
The bridge at Lower Bockhampton.

DORCHESTER AND THOMAS HARDY

(A circular ride around the lanes of the Frome Valley)

She turned in the high pew, until her sight
Swept the west gallery, and caught its row
Of music-men with viol, book and bow
Against the sinking sad tower-window light.
From *A Church Romance* by Thomas Hardy — set in Stinsford church

As its title suggests, this ride takes you through the small villages of the Frome Valley and visits places that have strong connections with the Victorian novelist and poet Thomas Hardy. He usually avoided using real place names in his novels and used his own substitutes — I have included these in brackets after the real name. This is a very pleasant, easy and relaxing ride that for the most part follows very quiet, unclassified country roads. The only section where you will meet a significant amount of traffic is leaving and re-entering Dorchester. After this you are mainly confined to minor country lanes running on either side of the River Frome. It is no surprise that Hardy drew so heavily on this part of Dorset for his inspiration, as he lived here for most of his life. He was born in 1840 at Higher Bockhampton (Upper Mellstock) in a house now known as Hardy's Cottage. Nearby Stinsford (Mellstock) also has strong Hardy connections. The church and its churchyard are particularly charming and typical of an old Dorset village. I would suggest detours to both Hardy's Cottage and Stinsford church (details below). Another possible detour is Rhododendron Drive which will be particularly attractive in May. This is on Puddletown Heath which is a small remainder of the once extensive Egdon Heath mentioned in *The Return of the Native.* Although the ride can be completed in two hours, I suggest that you make a day of it and enjoy visiting these places at a relaxed pace. Finally, Dorchester has two rail stations — Dorchester West is on the Heart of Wessex line which connects Dorchester with Bath and Bristol, and Dorchester South should be used for trains east to Wareham etc.

BACKGROUND AND PLACES OF INTEREST

Dorchester

Dorchester (Casterbridge) itself features very heavily in Hardy's work and many of its buildings are featured in his novels — *The Mayor of Casterbridge, Far from the Madding Crowd, The Trumpet-Major* and *Under the Greenwood Tree.* Although now a bustling town, Dorchester has a great deal of rural charm about it. There are many historic buildings in Dorchester itself, and as Hardy himself said: 'Casterbridge announced old Rome in every street, alley and precinct. It looked Roman, bespoke the art of Rome, concealed dead men of Rome.' You will find in High West Street: Judge Jeffrey's Lodging House, the Dorset County Museum and the original Old Crown Court where the Tolpuddle Martyrs were tried. Other attractions in the town are the Tutankhamun Exhibition, Dinosaur Museum, Hardy's Wessex Exhibition and the Dorset Military Museum.

Stinsford Church and Churchyard
The church and churchyard are only a very short detour from the route and here can be found the graves of Hardy's wife and immediate members of his family. However, only the heart of Hardy is buried here, laid to rest with his first wife. His ashes were interred in Westminster Abbey as a result of the popular wish of the time. There are further family memorials in the church and a stained glass window with an inscription to the writer. The church features in *Under the Greenwood Tree* and a number of poems. Also at rest is Cecil Day Lewis — the poet laureate — who was buried here at his own request because of his great admiration for Hardy. The church and churchyard attract a large number of literary enthusiasts.

Hardy's Cottage
This is situated at Higher Bockhampton. It is prominently signposted and only ½ mile from the cycle route. Hardy came from an ordinary country family and was born here in 1840. The cottage is picturesquely set in Puddletown Forest. It was built in 1801 by Hardy's grandfather and *Under the Greenwood Tree* and *Far from the Madding Crowd* were written here. It was acquired by the National Trust in 1947 and is open to the public on Sundays to Thursdays inclusive from April to October. At certain times queuing may be necessary. The site is very small and cars should be parked in the designated area, which is about a 10-minute walk from the cottage. The custodian's telephone number is 01305 262366.

Max Gate
Hardy returned to the Dorchester area after living for periods in London and Weymouth. He moved to Max Gate on the outskirts of Dorchester in 1885 and lived here until he died in 1928. The house was built by his brother to Hardy's own design. Max Gate is owned by the National Trust and the drawing room and garden are open to the public in the afternoons from April to September. The custodian's telephone number is 01305 262538.

Starting Point: This ride starts at the Wollaston Field long-term car park — see below.

Parking and Toilets: There are five long-stay car parks and four short-term car parks in Dorchester. You will save yourself some money if you select a long-term one. All of them are operated on a pay-and-display system. The car park closest to the start of this ride is the Wollaston Field long-term car park. This is near the Tudor Arcade shopping building which contains Waitrose, but the entrance to it is tucked away alongside the Dorset Day Centre. There is a public toilet in the Tudor Arcade building. If you wish to avoid parking in Dorchester there is an alternative car park near the route at Affpuddle Heath.

Travel by Rail: It is perfectly feasible to travel to the start of this ride by train as Dorchester has two separate stations on two different lines. Dorchester (West) is on the Heart of Wessex line that runs from Westbury to Weymouth. Dorchester (South) is on the Waterloo to Weymouth line. For details of carriage of cycles on these lines, please refer to the 'Transporting Cycles' chapter.

Distance: 16.3 miles circular.

Map: Ordnance Survey Landranger Sheet 194.

Hills: This ride is easy with no significant hills.

Nature of Route: One mile of this route at the start and end of this ride is on a fairly busy road that takes traffic into and out of Dorchester. Once you are clear of this, the majority of the ride is on very quiet country lanes. There are no off-road sections.

Safety: There are no particular hazards associated with this ride.

Refreshments: There is a large choice of places for refreshment in Dorchester. In addition, there is the Pine Lodge Farm Tea Room at 2.5 miles and the Wise Man Inn at West Stafford at 12.4 miles.

Nearest Tourist Information Centre: Unit 11, Antelope Walk, Dorchester, Dorset DT1 1BE (tel: 01305 267992).

Cycle Hire: Dorchester Cycles, 31 Great Western Road, Dorchester DT1 1UF (tel: 01305 268787).

Route Instructions:

1. (0.0 miles): From the Wollaston Field Car Park in Dorchester, proceed to the main street of Dorchester (High West Street) via Acland Road and Church Street and turn right by the traffic lights.

2. (0.5 miles): At the traffic lights by the bridge over the River Frome, proceed straight on.

3. (1.0 miles): At the roundabout marking the intersection with the bypass, go straight on as marked to 'Stinsford, Kingston Maurward, Bockhampton and Tincleton'. The fairly high level of traffic that you have experienced until now will ease off.

4. (7.3 miles): Turn right on to the busier B3390 as signposted to Weymouth.

5. (8.6 miles): Turn right at the cross-roads as directed to 'Woodsford 1¾, Dorchester 7'.

6. (11.7 miles): Turn right on to a busier road as directed to 'West Stafford ¾', and after a short distance on this road turn right again, to travel through the village.

7. (13.2 miles): The road will swing sharply left; at this point turn right as signposted 'Lower Bockhampton ½ mile'.

8. (14.2 miles): At the cross-roads turn left, signposted 'Stinsford ¾, Dorchester 2' and you will find yourself retracing the way that you took on your outward route.

9. (16.3 miles): Arrive back at your starting point.

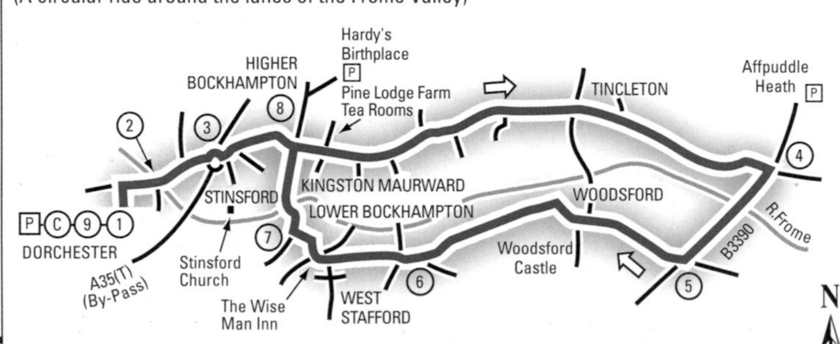

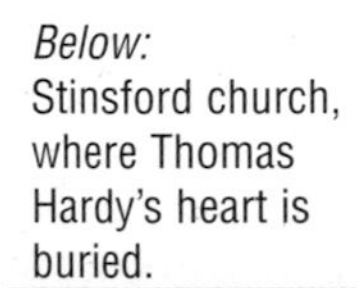
Below:
Stinsford church, where Thomas Hardy's heart is buried.

DORCHESTER AND THE TWO RIVERS

(A perfect escape to the downs following the Frome and Sydling rivers)

Any person wilfully injuring any part of this County Bridge will be guilty of felony, and upon conviction liable to be Transported for life. Early 19th century sign that still appears on several river bridges in the Dorchester area

Without doubt, the best cycle rides follow river valleys, as they usually provide a flat ride through villages of much interest, and this one is certainly no exception. The ride leaves the north side of Dorchester on the old Roman road that climbs fairly steeply above the Frome Valley, to pass the ancient earthworks of Poundbury Camp. Close to Stratton we cross the River Frome and the A356 to pick up the quietest of country lanes that almost touches the Sydling River all the way to Sydling St Nicholas and Up Sydling. Alternatively, instead of using the old Roman road and its rather hilly route past Poundbury Camp and Bradford Peverell, you can take a cycleway that follows the A37 all the way from Dorchester to Grimstone. I would recommend using the old Roman road on the outward leg and the cycleway for the return leg, and this is how I have described the route. There is a natural focal point for the ride and that is the Greyhound at Sydling St Nicholas, an excellent pub. Your alternative, if it is a nice day, is to take a picnic and follow one of a number of tracks that disappear into the downs above Up Sydling. However, I was unable to make it any further than Up Sydling due to the consumption of a pint or so of Addlestones cider in the Greyhound Inn, which led to the need for a premature afternoon nap.

BACKGROUND AND PLACES OF INTEREST

The Military Museum of Devon and Dorset

The museum is housed in the Keep, a Grade 2 listed building that you will see at the start of your ride. It was built in the 1870s as the gateway to the former barracks of the Dorsetshire Regiment. Spectacular views of the area can be seen from the battlements. The museum itself tells a fascinating story of those men who served in the regiments of Devon and Dorset from 1685 to the present day. Modern technology and creative displays help to tell the story of their traditions, courage, humour and sacrifice. Children are given activities to take part in to heighten their interest and enjoyment. Topical special exhibitions are run on a regular basis and there are also research facilities. School parties are welcome (tel: 01305 264066 for more information).

Above:
Poundbury Camp.

New Barn Field Centre

New Barn Field Centre is off the beaten track on the hill above the village of Bradford Peverell. It lies very close to the route, about 2 miles northwest of Dorchester on the A37 Yeovil road. The field centre is open to the public and adult or school parties are welcomed for all-day or part-day visits. There is also a residential study centre for school and youth groups in a carefully refurbished 18th century chalk and flint barn, stable and cart sheds. The centre houses exhibitions of traditional tools and equipment, a living history scene on how life was for our prehistoric ancestors in Wessex 2,000 years ago and a pottery where traditional skills are used to throw country-style stoneware products. Twenty acres of land have been given back to nature to create a traditional downland with wild flowers, ponds, hazel and ash coppice and picnic areas. There is also a selection of live animals to interest and delight young children. New Barn has a coffee shop with a restaurant (tel: 01305 268865 for more information).

The Dinosaur Museum

The Dinosaur Museum is situated on Icen Way, Dorchester, just off High East Street (A35) and is signposted from all the main car parks. It was awarded Dorset's Best Family Attraction in 1997. Young and old will be fascinated by the life-sized reconstructions, fossils, skeletons and audio-visual computerised and electronic displays which help to bring alive the incredible world of dinosaurs. Featured on TV, the museum will inform and entertain the family at any time of the year, whatever the weather! Open all year round, seven days a week (tel: 01305 269880 for more information).

Poundbury Camp

This Iron Age hill fort overlooking the River Frome is passed on the old Roman Road out of Dorchester. There is evidence of Bronze Age, Iron Age, Roman and later activities here. There is also some evidence of interesting Roman aqueducts that were constructed by the Roman army in the early part of the 1st century AD, and which were later adopted for civilian use. The fort was occupied by the military during the Napoleonic Wars, and during the 19th century Brunel proposed driving his railway through the area. This caused local outrage, led principally by William Barnes the Dorset dialect poet, and this ensured that the railway was routed through a tunnel. It was also the original reason for the formation of the County Archaeological Society.

Starting Point: This ride starts at the Top o' Town Car Park in Dorchester — see below.

Parking and Toilets: There are five long-stay car parks and four short-term car parks in Dorchester. You will save yourself some money if you select a long-term one. I parked in the Top o' Town Car Park (pay-and-display), which is the most conveniently situated for this ride. There are public toilets here and also a café. You could also park at the other end of the ride in Sydling St Nicholas, and make Dorchester the destination for your ride.

Travel by Rail: It is perfectly feasible to travel to the start of this ride by train as Dorchester has two separate stations on two different lines. Dorchester (West) is on the Heart of Wessex line that runs from Westbury to Weymouth. Dorchester (South) is on the Waterloo to Weymouth line. For details of carriage of cycles on these lines, please refer to the 'Transporting Cycles' chapter.

Distance: 17.2 miles.

Map: Ordnance Survey Landranger Sheet 194.

Hills: If you use the old Roman road through Bradford Peverell the first three miles of the ride are hilly. Thereafter there are no significant hills as you will be following the river valley.

Nature of Route: This ride takes place on very quiet, unclassified country roads and on a cycleway alongside the A37. There is a very short (0.3-mile) off-road section that could be muddy.

Safety: There are no particular hazards associated with this ride.

Refreshments: Plenty of choice in Dorchester. Also there is the Dragonfly at Grimstone (3.5 miles). I had a bite to eat at the Greyhound Inn at Sydling St Nicholas (7.3 miles) and it was excellent.

Nearest Tourist Information Centre: Unit 11, Antelope Walk, Dorchester, Dorset DT1 1BE (tel: 01305 267992).

Left:
A flowery bank at Bradford Peverell.

Cycle Hire: Dorchester Cycles, 31 Great Western Road, Dorchester, Dorset DT1 1UF (tel: 01305 268787).

Route Instructions:

1. (0.0 miles): From the Top o' Town Car Park in Dorchester start riding along Poundbury Road that starts by the Military Museum of Devon and Dorset. The road at first runs through an industrial estate, then past Poundbury Camp and on through Bradford Peverell.

Above:
The noticeboard at Poundbury Camp.

2. (3.1 miles): Turn right at the cross-roads to proceed over the bridge, to meet the main A37 road.

3. (3.3 miles): At the main road, by the little white cottage, cross the A37 (taking great care) and take the bridleway on the opposite side. Pass through a seven-bar metal gate and follow the right side of the field. Leave the field by the gate to continue in the same direction over the railway bridge.

4. (3.6 miles): When you meet the buildings of Grimstone Dairy, turn left to follow the concrete paved route (bridleway).

5. (3.9 miles): At the point where you are faced by the railway viaduct, turn right to follow a delightful country road that meanders parallel with the Sydling River.

6. (7.4 miles): Continue through Sydling St Nicholas and you will come to a junction, take the route signed 'Up Sydling 1'.

7. (7.8 miles): At the cross-roads, continue onward to Up Sydling along a road marked 'No through road for motor vehicles'.

8. (8.3 miles): At the fork by a small ford (may not flow in summer months) and Sydling Farm Fine Cheese and Farm Shop you have the choice of disappearing into the downs along one of the two tracks for a picnic, or starting your return journey to Dorchester. Assuming the latter, retrace your steps back to the point where you crossed the main A37 on the outward route.

9. (13.3 miles): At the A37, instead of retracing your route back through Bradford Peverell, follow the cycleway back towards Dorchester. The cycleway breaks at Stratton and you cycle through the village, picking it up again on the other side of the village. After that, the cycleway is continuous except for crossing to the other side of the A37.

10. (17.0 miles): The cycleway ends by Loders Garage and at this point you have to cycle or walk the short distance back to the Hardy Monument roundabout and turn right into Bridport Road for the car park.

11. (17.2 miles): Arrive back at the car park.

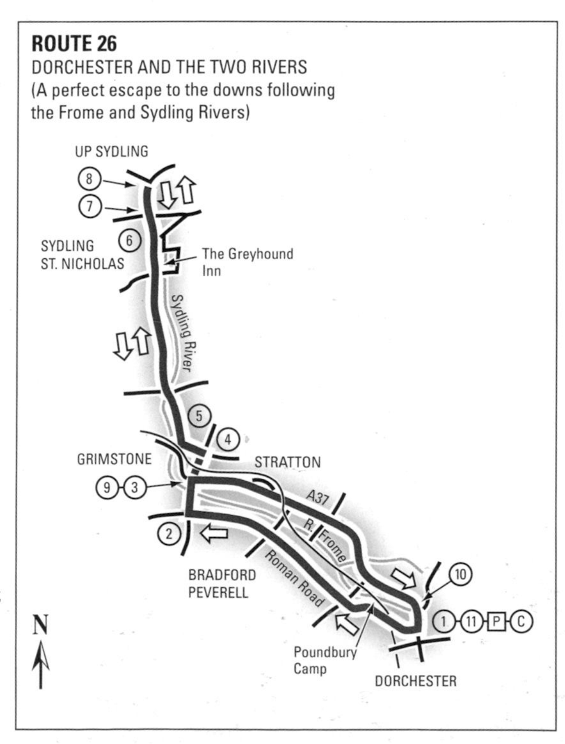

ROUTE 27

DORCHESTER AND THE HARDY MONUMENT

'The spot, however, is appropriate. It commands that English Channel Hardy did so much to defend; there is never a day when a British battleship cannot be seen from its summit.'
Sir Frederick Treves, writing in 1906, about the Hardy Monument in his *Highways and Byways in Dorset*

This ride takes as its theme the imposing monument on Black Down Hill. This part of Dorset is famous for people with the surname 'Hardy'. Dorchester is, of course, the home of Thomas Hardy, the great novelist. It is therefore surprising to someone from another county to find that the Hardy Monument, from where this ride starts, is nothing at all to do with Thomas Hardy the writer. It is in fact a memorial to Sir Thomas Masterman Hardy who was given command of Nelson's flagship HMS *Victory* in 1803 and led the ship when Nelson was struck down. Nelson is of course supposed to have cried 'Kiss me, Hardy' as he lay in Hardy's arms. After Nelson died, he brought the body home and took part in the grand funeral. Afterwards he became First Sea Lord and the Governor of Greenwich Hospital where he died in 1839. This circular ride starts in Dorchester and climbs steadily at first, but then after Martinstown climbs more steeply up to the monument on Black Down at 237m. The return leg meanders along a delightfully quiet lane at the foot of the south-facing downs, passing through a number of attractive and interestingly named hamlets like Coryates and Friar Waddon. To return to Dorchester without significant use of the busy A354 is essential and this has been achieved by briefly crossing the A354 to Bincombe, and then utilising a short stretch of the South West Coast Path (bridleway) before continuing to Dorchester on an unclassified road via Winterborne Herringston.

BACKGROUND AND PLACES OF INTEREST

The Hardy Monument

On Black Down, a hill some 234.7m above sea level, is a tower in memory of Nelson's Hardy. Although the sea cannot be seen from Thomas Masterman Hardy's boyhood home in Portesham, he used to love to climb the hills and look out over the English Channel that he did so much in later life to defend. Hardy always held in great regard everything that came from Dorset. When at sea he would claim that Dorset beer was 'the best ever drank', and that beer from 'Possum' was 'to be wholly commendable'. The monument was publicly funded in 1844 and has a spiral staircase with 120 steps that take you up the 21.3m to the top. Some writers have likened it to a factory chimney or a telephone receiver placed on its end and although I do not completely agree with this, it is definitely not the most graceful monument that I have seen adorning a hilltop. However, it makes up for this by its situation. Black Down on which it stands, although bare and desolate, provides such fine views of the countryside that was loved by Hardy in his boyhood and of the sea where he passed so much of his professional life.

Portesham

As well as being the birthplace of Thomas Masterman Hardy, the village of Portesham (or Portisham) which lies at the bottom of Black Down hill, topped by the Hardy Monument, also has famous prehistoric monuments. There is a group of nine upright stones supporting a huge single flat stone — a cromlech — called the Hell Stone. This was the burial spot of a chieftain of the late Stone Age. To the west lie another dolmen named 'The Grey Mare and Her Colts' and the Valley of Stones, a mysterious ravine in which many grey stones are scattered. The dead were carried for burial along this vale to a barrow some 16.4m long and 7.6m wide, once hidden under an earthen mound, but time and the intrusion of man have laid bare its stones.

Maiden Castle

You will notice to the south of your route, as you leave Dorchester, a very large earthwork known as Maiden Castle. The name is thought to have originated from Mai-Dun or Hill of Strength. It is one of the most impressive Celtic earthworks in England and stands on the summit of a hill, covering an area of 47 hectares.

Right:
The view from Black Down.

Opposite Left:
A cottage by the stream at Martinstown.

The earth defences follow the line of the hill and consist of at least three very steep ramparts 18m in height. Even now it is not easy to enter this fortress unless you make an entry by one of the four gate positions. At the time when it was built, it must have represented near perfection to the Celt. It had sufficient height that none could approach it unseen, grazing land all around for sheep and no undergrowth to hide wild animals. Below, alongside the River Frome, crops could be grown in the fertile land and fish could be caught, and no doubt the material to build mud and wattle huts could be found.

The County Museum, Dorchester

The County Museum is situated in the centre of Dorchester in High West Street and was founded in 1846. It was brought about as a result of the construction of the I. K. Brunel's railway line. Poundbury and many other important archaeological sites in the area were threatened, and a group of interested parties successfully negotiated with I. K. Brunel to change the route and this ensured their protection and also established the museum as an organisation for conservation. It contains one of Britain's finest prehistoric and Roman collections and there are also geological, archaeological, natural history and county history, art and literature sections (tel: 01305 262735 for more information or visit www.dorsetcountymuseum @dormus.demon.co.uk).

The Tutankhamun Exhibition

This exhibition has a superb collection of facsimiles of Tutankhamun's mummy and gold mask. Discover the ancient treasures of Egypt through an ingenious combination of sight, sound and smell that will leave you with an unforgettable experience. The exhibition is open daily, all year round (tel: 01305 269571 for more information).

Starting Point: This ride starts at the Fairfield long-term car park (see below).

Parking and Toilets: There are five long-stay car parks and four short-term car parks in Dorchester. You will save yourself some money if you select a long-term one. I parked in the Fairfield long-term car park (very low charges except on Wednesdays — market days). There are public toilets here. It is also possible to park at the Hardy Monument on Black Down. Public toilets can also be found at Upwey.

Travel by Rail: It is perfectly feasible to travel to the start of this ride by train as Dorchester has two separate stations on two different lines. Dorchester (West) is on the Heart of Wessex line that runs from Westbury to Weymouth. Dorchester (South) is on the Waterloo to Weymouth line. For details of the carriage of cycles on these lines, please refer to the 'Transporting Cycles' chapter.

Distance: 17.0 miles.

Map: Ordnance Survey Landranger Sheet 194.

Hills: This is one of the most energetic rides in the book. Obviously, one of the highest hills in Dorset can not be mastered without a little exercise and the climb from Dorchester to the monument is about 180m.

Nature of Route: An exhilarating hilly ride that starts off with a stiff climb up Black Down followed by a fast descent to Portesham. The vast majority (13 miles) is on unclassified roads, 3 miles is on B roads, about half a mile on an A road, and there is a half-mile off-road section (distances are approximate).

Safety: The fast downhill section to Portesham demands the use of a helmet. Care should be taken on the A354, especially when leaving it on a sharp bend to take the road to Bincombe. I would advise dismounting here.

Refreshments: There is a large choice of places for refreshment in Dorchester. En route there is the Brewers Arms in Martinstown, the Kings Arms at Portesham and the Masons Arms at Upwey.

Nearest Tourist Information Centre: Unit 11, Antelope Walk, Dorchester, Dorset DT1 1BE (tel: 01305 267992).

Cycle Hire: Dorchester Cycles, 31 Great Western Road, Dorchester, Dorset DT1 1UF (tel: 01305 268787).

Route Instructions:

1. (0.0 miles): From the Fairfield Car Park in Dorchester, turn left into Fairfield Road and then right into Maumbury Road, and at the traffic lights turn left to go under the railway bridge (as directed to Bridport).

2. (0.2 miles): At the traffic lights just after the railway bridge, proceed straight on into Damers Road with the Dorset County Hospital on your right.

3. (0.7 miles): Bear left at the end of Damers Road, where it meets Bridport Road, and carry straight on at the next two small roundabouts.

4. (1.6 miles): When you come to the roundabout marking the intersection with the Dorchester bypass, take the second exit which is a small road marked 'Martinstown 1¾'.

5. (2.9 miles): Turn right at the give-way junction as directed to 'Steepleton 1¼, Hardy's Monument 2¼, Bridport 12½'.

6. (3.6 miles): Just as you are leaving Martinstown, turn left as indicated to 'Hardy's Monument 2'.

7. (6.5 miles): Turn left as signposted to Portesham and Abbotsbury and after a short distance you will be able to enjoy an exhilarating run down Portesham Hill.

8. (7.6 miles): Brake hard so that you manage to take the left turn by the church in Portesham as directed to 'Coryates, Friar Waddon and Upwey'.

9. (11.4 miles): By Bayard Dairy turn right on to the B3159, as indicated 'Weymouth 4'.

10. (11.9 miles): In Upwey, turn left on to a narrow road marked 'Unsuitable for Heavy Goods Vehicles'.

11. (12.2 miles): Taking great care, turn left on to the main Dorchester/Weymouth road (A354). This is a very busy road with heavy vehicles, but you will be on it for only a short distance.

12. (12.5 miles): Almost immediately after passing under the railway line, on a very sharp bend, leave the A354 by turning right, into a lane marked 'To Bincombe only'. Take very great care when making the right turn — it would be best to dismount.

13. (13.2 miles): Just after entering Bincombe, take a bridleway on the left marked 'Inland Coast Path, Came Wood and Hardy Monument'. This turning is by Granary House, and initially has a tarmac surface but then becomes a green lane. Follow this lane until you come to a metal barred gate marking the availability of a surfaced road again.

14. (14.0 miles): Leave the green lane via the gate and take the road straight on with the golf course on the left and wood on the right, to travel mainly downhill back to Dorchester through Winterborne Herringston.

15. (16.7 miles): At the junction of Herringston Road with Maumbury Road and South Court Avenue, follow Maumbury Road.

16. (16.8 miles): At the traffic lights, continue along Maumbury Road, and you will see the car park on the right.

17. (17.0 miles): Arrive back at Fairfield long-term car park.

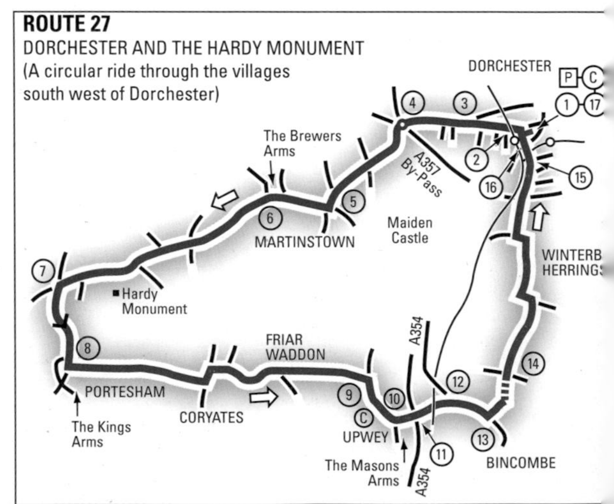

ROUTE 27
DORCHESTER AND THE HARDY MONUMENT
(A circular ride through the villages south west of Dorchester)

Left:
The Yetminster old Boyles School nameplate.

THE HEART OF WESSEX LINE

(A ride from Yetminster to Maiden Newton with the option of returning by the Heart of Wessex railway line)

Yetminster, the chief place near Sherborne, is a picturesque townlet, full of quaint old houses and venerable thatched cottages. The dates on the buildings belong mostly to the early part of the seventeenth century. In the main street is an old thatch-roofed inn, as well as many houses in ancient stone with stone-mullioned windows and fine gables.
Sir Frederick Treves, writing in 1906, in his *Highways and Byways in Dorset*

This ride is a linear one that takes you from the old but sizeable village of Yetminster to Maiden Newton. A linear ride of 16½ miles, that is made possible by the existence of railway stations at both of these settlements. The stations are connected by the Heart of Wessex line, which enables you to return directly from Maiden Newton to Yetminster by rail without changing trains. However, if you do not wish to take advantage of the railway, there is a second option of a circular ride from Yetminster that is, by sheer co-incidence, exactly the same length. This shares the same route initially, as far as Holywell, but then returns to Yetminster via Chetnole. I rode both routes on a bright sunny day in May, when the countryside was probably at its best. I have never seen or smelt so much wild garlic in a short space of time as I did on that day — it was glorious. There are plenty of pubs for refreshment around the route, and the Sutton Bingham Reservoir provides a good picnic opportunity.

BACKGROUND AND PLACES OF INTEREST

The Heart of Wessex Line

I must confess to a small vested interest in the Heart of Wessex line. The line runs from Bristol to Weymouth and calls at 18 stations in between. It is very much a branch line — single track in places — and you get this feeling that it is just about surviving by the skin of its teeth. There is also a peculiar charm about the line — passengers at village stations must hold out their arms to request the driver to stop, and most of the railway staff have worked on the line for many years. My vested interest arises from the fact that in the autumn of 1999, the Bristol to Weymouth Rail Partnership (an alliance of Wales & West Passenger Trains and local councils) decided to hold a competition to name the line. The competition was run by BBC Radio Bristol, and two entrants came up with the winning name — Roger Porch of Keynsham and myself. The name now appears on a publicity leaflet for the line and, hopefully over the next few years, it will start to appear on some station signboards. As far as practical issues are concerned, there are up to eight trains a day in each direction on Mondays to Saturdays with a service on summer Sundays and some winter Sundays as well. The line forms a very useful facility for cyclists as bikes can be carried on the trains, making a linear ride possible and providing a comfortable return for tired legs to your starting point. However, the modern railcar units have restricted space and carriage of bikes is at the discretion of the conductor if the train is crowded. The line also has a website (www.heartofwessex.org.uk). See the 'Transporting Cycles' chapter for further information.

Yetminster

The character and old-fashioned feel of the centre of this village, situated on the River Wriggle, has been retained because there is very little evidence of modern building and little through traffic. There is a surprisingly large number of 17th century buildings, many built from local yellow-orange limestone with stone-mullioned windows and gables. There are also many thatched cottages, including the inn in the main street. The 15th century Minster of St Andrew is a fine church and provides a uniquely royalist environment for the local residents as the national anthem rings out no less than six times a day. Unfortunately, this means some hard work for the person who has to climb the 50 or so steps into the belfry and wind up the three movements. Yetminster Fair is one of the biggest and oldest fairs in Dorset. It was started in the 13th century under a charter granted by the Bishop of Salisbury. Although the fair lapsed in 1947, it was restarted in 1975 and is now held on the second Saturday in July.

Maiden Newton

This is a large chalk-stream village that lies at the confluence of the rivers Hooke and Frome. The latter river divides the village into two parishes — Frome Vauchurch on the west bank of the River Frome and Maiden Newton on the east. It has a mixture of old and new buildings but its history goes back much further than these buildings tell. In prehistoric times, Maiden Newton was at the junction of four ancient trackways, of which the Wessex Ridgeway is still in use today. The village is also the site of a Roman house with a beautiful mosaic pavement. The mosaic depicts many portraits of pagan gods and a picture of Neptune in conflict with sea monsters, with a border of dogs chasing deer. In one corner there is a cross, probably put there by a Christian mason. The village was also mentioned in the Domesday Book. The church of St Mary is basically medieval with the main part being 15th century. Interestingly, in the north wall is a blocked doorway that has one of the oldest original doors in England. Made in 1450, studded with nails and hanging on its original hinges, it locks with a wooden bar placed in stone grooves in the wall. The church also bears bullet holes. The first came from a gun fired by one of Cromwell's men during the Civil War, and the second penetrated the window above the altar and was fired from a German aircraft during World War 2. Unfortunately, the tourist interest in Maiden Newton declined when the 17th century White Hart Inn was demolished.

Starting Point: This ride starts from the High Street in Yetminster — see below.

Parking and Toilets: Despite trying very hard, I was unable to find a car park in Yetminster. The streets are rather narrow as befits a 17th century village, so my best advice is to park near the post office where the High Street is at its widest. As your car will be located there for several hours please park it to minimise disruption to the village. It is also possible to arrive by rail — the Heart of Wessex line will take you, without changing, towards Bath and Bristol in one direction and Dorchester and Weymouth in the other. For further details, see the 'Transporting Cycles' chapter. The only public convenience that I could locate was at Sutton Bingham.

Distance: Both the linear and circular routes are 16.5 miles long.

Map: Ordnance Survey Landranger Sheet 194

Hills: This ride is in undulating chalk country with one or two climbs around Cattistock, but otherwise no arduous hills.

Nature of Route: This ride takes place entirely on surfaced roads, all of which are quiet and unclassified.

Safety: It is necessary to cross the A37 in two places: at Ryme Intrinseca and at Holywell. The A37 is a very fast road and great care should be taken when crossing. I would advise dismounting in both cases. The crossing at Holywell is particularly dangerous and is also wider, with three lanes to cross.

Refreshments: There is the White Hart in Yetminster, a pleasant-looking pub. In Evershot there is the Acorn Inn — a pub with strong Hardy connections. At around 15 miles there is the Fox and Hounds at Cattistock. For those doing the circular ride, there is the Chetnole Inn at Chetnole (14 miles).

Nearest Tourist Information Centre: 3 Tilton Court, Digby Road, Sherborne, Dorset DT9 3NL (tel: 01935 815341).

Right:
The old Boyles School at Yetminster.

Cycle Hire: Yeovil Cycle Centre, Western Terrace, Yeovil (tel: 01935 422000) and Dorset Cycle Hire (tel: 01963 362476).

Route Instructions:

1. (0.0 miles): Cycle up the High Street in Yetminster, to pass the White Hart pub, and at the end of the High Street, turn left and then immediately right into Ryme Road.

2. (1.9 miles): After Ryme Intrinseca, carefully cross the A37 and take the no through road (marked as suitable for cyclists and horses with a green sign). Continue on the very short cycleway to rejoin the lane to Netherton.

3. (3.1 miles): Shortly after passing the Sutton Bingham Treatment Works, turn left at the give-way junction as directed to 'Sutton Bingham ½, East Coker 1'.

4. (5.7 miles): In Halstock, take a left turn (unmarked at the time of riding); the turning is opposite St Juthware Close.

5. (6.6 miles): Turn right at the give-way junction as directed to 'Chelborough 1¼, Evershot 3¼, Rampisham 3¾'.

6. (8.5 miles): At the staggered cross-roads, turn left as signposted to Evershot.

7. (8.9 miles): At this give-way junction turn left (the signpost was broken at the time of riding) to descend into Evershot.

On reaching the junction with the A37 at Holywell there are two alternatives — you can either cycle to Maiden Newton and return by the Heart of Wessex line to Yetminster, or cycle a circular route via Chetnole back to Yetminster. Instructions 8 to 12 are for the rail option, and A to D are for the circular option.

8. (11.3 miles): Take extreme care at this junction with the A37 as it is a three-lane trunk road and traffic moves very fast. Turn right for a short distance on the A37 and take the next right to Frome St Quintin and Chantmarle. I would strongly advise that you should dismount from your arrival at the A37 until you have safely gained access to the lane to Frome St Quintin.

9. (14.2 miles): Bear right as indicated to Maiden Newton and Cattistock.

10. (14.4 miles): At the Sandhills Junction (GR 589003) bear left as indicated to Cattistock and Maiden Newton.

11. (16.3 miles): In Maiden Newton, at the end of Cattistock Road you will come to a stop junction. Cross into Station Road, which as you would expect takes you to the railway station for your return to Yetminster.

12. (16.5 miles): Arrive at the station.

A. (11.3 miles): Take extreme care at this junction with the A37 as it is a three-lane trunk road and traffic moves very fast. Cross the A37 (I would strongly advise that you should dismount to do this) and take the route signposted to 'Batcombe 2¼, Minterne Magna 5' and then immediately left to Batcombe, Melbury Bubb and Chetnole.

B. (12.7 miles): Turn left between a thatched cottage and a white house (named Redford). There is a signpost (GR 606057) but it was hidden and broken at the time of riding. No directions are necessary between here and Yetminster.

C. (16.2 miles): In Yetminster, turn right into the High Street to return to your starting point.

D. (16.5 miles): Arrive back at the post office.

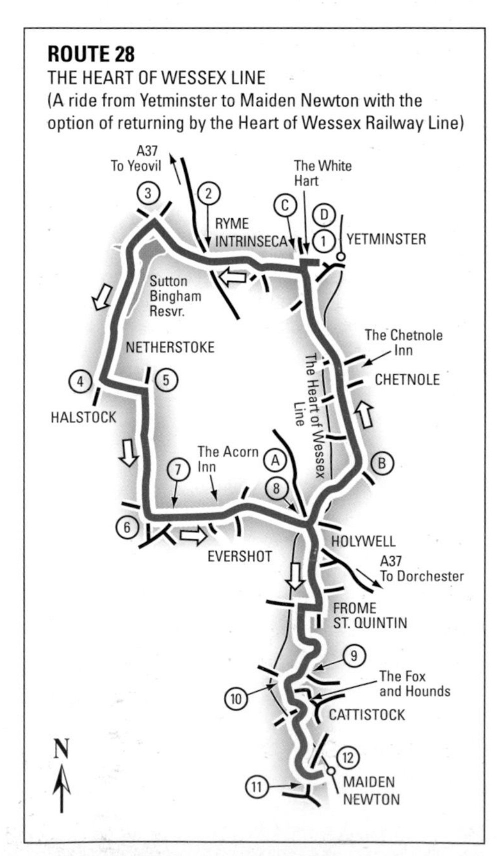

ROUTE 29

ABBOTSBURY TO BURTON BRADSTOCK

(An inland route connecting two of Dorset's coastal beauty spots)

Like an inconsequent dream is a walk about this happy place, so strangely are Past and Present mixed in it.

An observation on Abbotsbury from *Arthur Mee's The King's England — Dorset*, first published in 1939

Once having climbed Portesham Hill, given a fine day, you will find the views of the sea, Chesil Beach and Portland truly inspiring. You will feel as if you are on the roof of the world. Unfortunately, these pleasures do not come without a little pain and the initial climb up Portesham Hill is indeed a steep one. After this, the outward leg is easy with a gradual descent following the course of the small River Bride — although the river is rarely seen by the cyclist and you might not realise the existence of the stream. There are two possibilities for the return from Burton Bradstock to Abbotsbury. The instructions route you back along the B3157. This is a road with many short sharp hills and quite a lot of traffic and if you would prefer to avoid this traffic then I would recommend returning via your outward route. Although neither option takes in the Abbotsbury Swannery, it is worth a visit if you have young children, especially if you are there when the young swans are hatching in May and June.

BACKGROUND AND PLACES OF INTEREST

Abbotsbury Village

Abbotsbury is a little touristy but what there is has been done tastefully. It is at the western end of Chesil Beach and is a picturesque village with stone-built 16th and 17th century thatched or tiled cottages, and houses of the same period with heavy buttresses and stone-mullioned windows. Little of the Benedictine abbey, founded in the reign of Canute by Orca (a steward of the king) and his wife Tola, and once the glory of Abbotsbury, has survived, but there is evidence of its existence all around. For example, some of the domestic buildings have been turned into farmhouses and cottages. Blocks of stone, fragments of church carvings or even part of a Gothic arch have been used in some of the buildings and a gatehouse and archway still stand. The most impressive building that remains is the enormous 84m barn, part of which is still thatched. The abbey flourished for 500 years but when the monasteries were broken up, the land passed to Sir Giles Strangways and the buildings fell into decay. A mansion was built from their stones and the Strangways lived here until the Civil War when it was garrisoned for the king. In September 1644 Sir Anthony Ashley Cooper, at the head of the Parliamentary force, attacked the village, took the church and burnt down the house. In the oak pulpit of the church can still be seen two holes made by bullets from Cromwell's men. In one of the stained glass windows in the

Below:
The cliffs at Burton Bradstock.

chancel is a faded woman's head. The beautiful, wistful face is reputed to be that of St Catherine and to the southwest of the village, on the crown of a hill, is the chapel of this very saint. It is small, about 14m by 5m, and is a fine example of the Perpendicular period of architecture.

Abbotsbury Swannery, Sub-Tropical Gardens, Children's Farm and Terracotta Warriors

There are four separate attractions around the village of Abbotsbury. The Swannery, a sanctuary for over 600 free flying swans, was voted Dorset's best family attraction in 1999. During late May and June hundreds of baby swans will be hatching. Visitors can help to feed the swans every day, at 12 noon and 4pm. The Swannery also has an audiovisual show, a self-service coffee shop and a gift shop. It is open from Easter until October (tel: 01305 871858 for more information).

The Sub-Tropical Gardens are open most days of the year. The first Countess of Ilchester established a kitchen garden here in 1765. Over the years the gardens have been developed and extended into an 8-hectare site with rare and exotic plants from all over the world. Today it is a Grade 1 listed garden with a mixture of formal and informal planting. There are walled garden walks, many suitable for wheelchairs, and spectacular woodland valley views and ancient lily ponds. There is a self-service café, a gift shop and a nursery stocked with quality plants. Events are held here all year (tel: 01305 871387 for more information).

The Tithe Barn Children's Farm and Terracotta Warriors display is a wonderful place for young children. They can cuddle rabbits and guinea pigs, bottle-feed lambs, milk cows, race toy tractors, feed doves and touch donkeys and horses. The Terracotta Warriors are on display in the barn and a visit is included in the price of the ticket. It is open from Easter until October (tel: 01305 871817 for more information).

Burton Bradstock

Burton Bradstock is a fishing village. The River Bride flows past the church on its way to the end of Chesil Beach. The church is about 500 years old and has some notable features but it is the manor that has a more interesting history. The manor was the price Henry I had to pay to the Abbey of Caen to redeem the Conqueror's crown and jewels. How these treasures happened to be in the possession of the monks is not clear, but it was claimed by them that William had bequeathed them to the monks on his deathbed. It was only when the gift of Burton Bradstock was offered that the monks could be persuaded to surrender them back to the King.

Starting Point: This ride starts from the public car park in Abbotsbury (for details see below).

Parking and Toilets: Park in the public car park in Abbotsbury where there is usually a small charge. This is on the Portesham side of the village close to the tithe barn and abbey ruins. The entrance is opposite Rosemary Lane. There is also a small car park at Bishops Lime Kiln picnic area. There are also car parks at Burton Bradstock and a public toilet opposite the Texaco garage in Burton.

Distance: 18.5 miles if you return via the B3157. If you return via the same route as your outward route the distance is 23.2 miles.

Maps: Ordnance Survey Landranger Sheets 193 and 194.

Hills: There is an extremely steep climb at the beginning of the ride that lifts you up on to the downs. Thereafter there are no serious hills on the outward route to Burton Bradstock. If you return to Abbotsbury using your outward route in reverse, there is a steady almost imperceptible climb over the 6 miles to Littlebredy and then a steeper climb to Portesham Hill. If you return via the B3157 then you will find the route can also be tiring as it is made up of many short climbs.

Nature of Route: The outward leg of this ride takes place over extremely quiet country lanes and is a delightful experience. The return leg is via the B3157 — a road that is a little too busy for perfect cycling. The option of retracing the route to Abbotsbury via your outward route is one that you should consider.

Safety: If you have young children cycling with you, then it would be best to avoid using the B3157 for the return leg as it is narrow in places and can be busy at times.

Refreshments: In Abbotsbury there is the Swan Inn, the Ilchester Arms, various tea rooms and also a cafeteria at the Swannery. At Litton Cheney there is the White Horse Inn and also a tea room. In Burton Bradstock there is the 17th century Dove Inn. There are beach cafés in Burton Bradstock, and in Swyre there is the Bull Inn.

Nearest Tourist Information Centre: Unit 11, Antelope Walk, Dorchester, Dorset DT1 1BE (tel: 01305 267992).

Cycle Hire: Dorchester Cycles, 31 Great Western Road, Dorchester DT1 1UF (tel: 01305 268787).

Route Instructions:

1. (0.0 miles): Leave the Abbotsbury car park by crossing the B3157 into Rosemary Lane. At the end of this short lane, turn right into Hands Lane to make the stiff climb up Portesham Hill.

2. (2.3 miles): At the Portesham Hill crossroads (GR 602874), turn left toward Winterbourne Abbas and Dorchester.

3. (2.7 miles): Turn left down a narrow lane (at the time of riding the signpost was missing).

4. (3.6 miles): Turn left to descend the 14% hill to Littlebredy. After the village you will pass between two stone pillars — do not worry as this is not a private drive.

5. (5.8 miles): At the Long Bredy Junction (GR 569900), turn left as signposted to Puncknowle 3, Swyre 3¾ and Kingston Russell House. Almost immediately at a further junction, swing right as signposted to Litton Cheney and Bridport.

6. (7.2 miles): At the junction by the youth hostel and the White Horse Inn, turn left as signposted to Bridport. At this point there is also an additional signpost to Puncknowle, Burton Bradstock and Bridport.

Above:
Abbotsbury village.

7. (11.1 miles): At the junction with the B3157 (by Larkfield Caravan Park) turn right to cycle into Burton Bradstock.

8. (11.4 miles): Turn left into Cliff Road and cycle to the end to enjoy the views from Burton Cliffs. Alternatively, you can carry on a little further into the centre of the village.

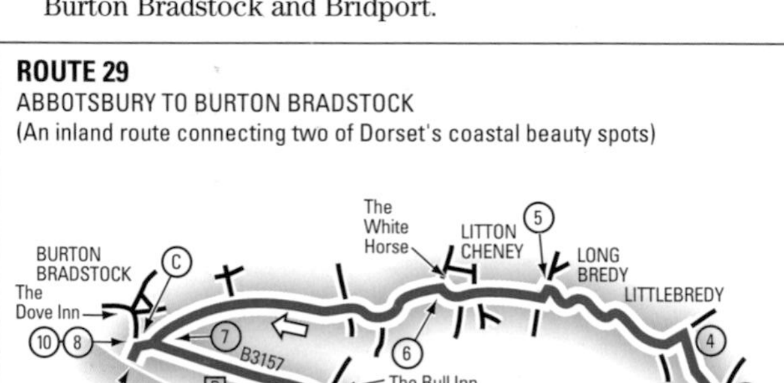

9. (11.6 miles): Assuming you have turned left for the clifftop, having enjoyed the views of the Dorset coast and Portland, to return to Abbotsbury you can either retrace your outward route, or return along the B3157 to Abbotsbury. The remaining, very simple, instructions assume a return via the B3157.

10. (11.8 miles): At the foot of Cliff Road, turn right along the B3157 and keep on this busy road all the way back to Abbotsbury.

11. (18.5 miles): Arrive back at your starting point at the car park at Abbotsbury.

Above:
West Bay harbour.

THE BRIT VALLEY

(Following the River Brit from Beaminster to the sea)

I rode from Britport 3. Miles to Netherbyri, and then a mile farther to Bemistre. The ground al this way is in an exceeding good and almost the best vain of ground for corne, and pasture, and wood that is in al Dorsetshire.

From John Leland's *Itinerary* written between 1535 and 1543, as he toured England and Wales on behalf of King Henry VIII, rescuing important books for the Royal Library from the collections being broken up by the dissolution of the monasteries

I was really looking forward to this ride as it is many years since, as a child, I was taken to West Bay with my family on summer day trips. I remember that I used to play for hours in the wind-blown sand and very fine shingle. I was not to be disappointed as this ride turned out to be a perfect gem. It starts inland in Beaminster and journeys due south via Netherbury to Bridport and then West Bay, so we have the seaside as a natural destination for our ride. The journey roughly follows the course of the River Brit as it makes its way to the sea. It is therefore a mainly flat ride with just a couple of climbs. Apart from each end of the ride, at Beaminster and West Bay, the route is very rural and follows the quietest of country lanes. I rode the route early one sunny June morning, and memories of the banks and hedgerows lined with sweet-scented wild honeysuckle and the more pungently scented elderflowers come back to mind, together with the occasional sighting of the swift-flowing River Brit. If you have children in your party you will need to allow time to explore the harbour and cliffs of West Bay, and to play on the beach where the coarse sand and very fine shingle are still to be found.

ROUTE 30
THE BRIT VALLEY
(Following the River Brit from Beaminster to the sea)

BEAMINSTER
1 12 P
C
2
4
3
Parnham House
NETHERBURY
5
6
The Hare and Hounds
WAYTOWN
River Brit
7
The Pyemore Inn
8
BRIDPORT
9
A35(T)
10
11
WEST BAY
N

BACKGROUND AND PLACES OF INTEREST

Beaminster

To many Beaminster will be known as Emminster, the 'hill-surrounded little town' of Thomas Hardy's Tess. Beaminster (pronounced Beminster) is a prosperous old market town which once thrived from wool, cloth including sailcloth and sackcloth, shoe-thread, rope and twine. Due to the devastation caused by three fires, first in 1644 during the Royalist occupation, then again in 1684 and 1781, few of the old houses survive. However, the whole of the town's historic centre is a conservation area with over 200 listed buildings. There are charming places in the town to browse, shop or to sample the local fare such as the famous Blue Vinny cheese, without which, it is said, no Dorset man is really happy. Thomas Hine, who gave his name to Cognac Hine, which is recognised as being the connoisseur's cognac, was born in Beaminster in 1775. In 1792 he left to seek his fortune in France where he found employment in the brandy business in Jarnac. There he married the boss's daughter, became a partner and finally owned the business, giving the company his name. The church tower in Beaminster was built in 1520 and is one of the finest in the country. It is a tower of many pinnacles, gargoyles and niches. There are carvings of the Virgin Mary, the Crucifixion, the Resurrection and the Ascension. From this magnificent tower some of Monmouth's followers were hanged in 1685. Around Beaminster are some notable houses including Parnham and Mapperton.

Parnham House and Gardens

These are open to the public from April until October and can be visited on this ride via a very short detour. The house is a beautiful, large Tudor mansion that belonged to the Strode family for many generations. There are striking sculptures of members of the Strode family in the church. Now it is the home of John and Jennie Makepeace who have lovingly restored and enlivened this wonderful house and created their own internationally famous John Makepeace Furniture Studio (tel: 01308 862204 for more information).

Starting Point: This ride starts from the Yarn Barton Car Park in Beaminster (see below).

Mapperton House

Situated about 2 miles southeast of Beaminster, this is one of the most famous houses of Dorset, dating from the reign of Henry VIII. One family, through the female line, has retained the grand house, built in warm grey-yellow stone with balustrade parapet and dormer windows, for many generations. The garden surrounds the manor house and is an area of outstanding natural beauty. It has been used several times as a location in films including *Emma* and *Tom Jones*. The Italianate walled gardens were laid out by Mrs Ethel Labouchère in memory of her husband. A classical orangery was built in 1966 and stands at the head of the valley. The formal gardens fall in descending levels down to the valley, the ponds giving way to a grassy walk edged with beautiful trees that gradually fade away into the Dorset countryside. The gardens are open to the public from March to October (tel: 01308 862645 for further information).

Bridport

Bridport was, in the 13th century, the focus for the rope and net-making industry. Today it has good shops and a thriving market, is the largest town in West Dorset and is still Britain's main source of twine. The long, straight alleys in the town were once 'rope walks', where twine and rope were laid out in long lengths extending from the backs of houses as part of a cottage industry. The peak of the town's prosperity was in the 18th and 19th centuries when many of the houses which can still be seen in South Street were built. Nets made in Bridport are used by fishing fleets all over the world. In more recent years, a local company has made tennis nets for Wimbledon and nets for the Space Shuttle. Buildings in the town of historical interest are the medieval church and chantry, the Tudor museum and the Georgian town hall. Britain's only thatched brewery, Palmers of Bridport, is a traditional, family-run business that has been in existence for over 200 years. It is situated on the banks of the river, on the southern edge of town. Bridport Museum is in the centre of town, and was reopened in April 2000. The Ropemaker's Apprentice guides visitors through the history of Saxon Bridport (tel: 01308 422116 for more information).

Parking and Toilets: There is a car park in The Square, although it is probably better to park where I did in the Yarn Barton Car Park just a short distance away. Other parking opportunities exist in Bridport and West Bay. All these parking places have public toilets.

Distance: 16.8 miles.

Map: Ordnance Survey Landranger Sheet 193.

Hills: For the most part, this ride is flat as it follows the Brit Valley, and there are only a couple of climbs where the route is fairly steep.

Nature of Route: This ride has an initial off-road element and after this it mostly takes place on country lanes following the Brit Valley. There is some urban cycling between Bridport and West Bay.

Safety: There are no significant safety hazards associated with this ride.

Refreshments: You will find a good choice of pubs and tea rooms in Beaminster, Bridport and West Bay. En route you will find the Hare & Hounds in Waytown at 3 miles and the Pyemore Inn at 4 miles.

Nearest Tourist Information Centre: 32 South Street, Bridport, Dorset DT6 3NQ (tel: 01308 424901).

Cycle Hire: There seems to be no cycle hire facility in the Bridport or Beaminster areas. The nearest cycle hire shop appears to be Dorchester Cycles, 31 Great Western Road, Dorchester, Dorset DT1 1UF (tel: 01305 268787).

Route Instructions:

1. (0.0 miles): Leave the Yarn Barton Car Park in Beaminster and you will come to the Market Place. Take the little narrow road called Church Street and then almost immediately turn into St Mary Well Street. Where the road ends continue along the Brit Valley Way. The route then becomes an unsealed gravel track and you soon meet a gate. Avoid the more obvious route left which is a private drive, but swing right around the right-hand side of the wood on the bridleway — this has the appearance of a field path. Continue along this across the sloping field.

2. (0.6 miles): You will come to a wooden kissing gate alongside a metal gate. Pass through this into the next field.

3. (0.9 miles): The next gate is at the edge of the wood. Take the right-hand route here (the left-hand route will take you down and across the river to enjoy Parnham House and Gardens if you wish) and continue along the edge of the wood on a track that can be muddy at times.

4. (1.1 miles): At the junction with the unsealed stony track, bear half-left to join it. After the track descends the hill you need to be careful to spot the right turn through the six-bar metal gate. Go through the gate and then left away from the decaying Dutch barns. You will swing right, up a steep hill between high banks toward the surfaced road in Netherbury.

5. (1.8 miles): You will meet the surfaced road close to the church at a property called Millstones. Turn left here toward the village of Netherbury.

6. (1.9 miles): Turn right as directed to Waytown and Bridport.

7. (4.8 miles): At the give-way junction, turn left as signposted to Bridport — you also join the National Cycleway Route 2 at this point — and then after about 300yd, turn right to continue on the National Cycleway (signposted Pyemore and Bridport).

8. (6.5 miles): The peace and tranquillity of the ride come to an end as you meet West Street in Bridport, opposite the Ropemakers pub. Turn left here toward the town clock and then right at the traffic lights to turn into South Street.

9. (7.1 miles): At the traffic lights adjacent to Palmers Brewery, go straight on as indicated to 'West Bay (all routes)'.

10. (7.2 miles): At the Bridport bypass roundabout take the third exit into West Bay Road (on the right side of the Crown Inn).

11. (8.4 miles): Arrive at West Bay to enjoy the fresh sea air and explore the beach, cliffs and harbour. The return route simply retraces the outward route.

12. (16.8 miles): Arrive back at Yarn Barton Car Park in Beaminster.

CYCLING INITIATIVES BY PUBLIC BODIES

The purpose of this section is to provide you with information that will enable you to develop further rides in addition to the 30 rides provided in this book. I have therefore restricted the routes to the better known and longer leisure routes and have not included utility cycle routes provided by district councils or unitary authorities. The list is not exhaustive — cycling is increasing in popularity and new publications come into print all the time, while others fall by the wayside.

DORSET

The North Dorset Cycleway: This route is maintained by Dorset County Council and North Dorset District Council. It is a circular route of 73 miles with some linking routes that make shorter day rides possible. The circular route is currently signposted in only one direction (anti-clockwise), but it is hoped to signpost the route in both directions in the near future. However, the linking routes are signed in both directions. The route utilises quiet country lanes and passes through picturesque villages and old market towns. Although the section through Blackmoor Vale is fairly flat, this changes when the route passes over the Dorset Downs, where there are some challenging climbs. When you ride the day rides in this book, the brown signs with the blue disks will become quite familiar to you as the routes inevitably share their course with the cycleway, looking for the quietest and safest possible lanes. Access to the route by rail is possible from Gillingham station which is on the Waterloo to Exeter line. Leaflets are available from local tourist information centres or by contacting Cycling, Environmental Services Directorate, County Hall, Dorchester, Dorset DT1 1XJ (tel: 01305 224558). Information can also be found by visiting www.dorset-cc.gov.uk.

The Purbeck Cycleway: This route is maintained by Dorset County Council and Purbeck District Council. The main circular route is 47 miles long and takes in a wide variety of landscape, much of which is hilly. It passes through Wareham, Bere Regis, West Lulworth and Corfe Castle. There are two loops of 12 miles and one of 22 miles that make shorter day rides possible. Part of the route runs over army ranges, but these are usually open during August and most weekends. When this section is closed there is an alternative route available that avoids the range. If you wish to check whether the range is open, contact either Wareham Tourist Information Centre (tel: 01929 552740) or Swanage Tourist Information Centre (tel: 01929 422885). Access to the cycleway is possible by rail from Wareham, Wool and Moreton. Leaflets are available from local tourist information centres or by contacting Cycling, Environmental Services Directorate, County Hall, Dorchester, Dorset DT1 1XJ (tel: 01305 224558). Information can also be found by visiting www.dorset-cc.gov.uk.

The Castleman Trailway: This route is shorter and flatter than the previous two and follows the old 'Castleman's Corkscrew' railway line. It runs for 16 miles from Upton Country Park near Poole to the River Avon at Ringwood. At present, it is only fully open to walkers, and cyclists have to seek an alternative route over the section from Dolman's Crossing to West Moors. Access to the trailway is possible from Poole railway station. Leaflets are available from local tourist information centres or by contacting Dorset County Council's Countryside Service Eastern Offices (tel: 01425 478082). Information can also be found by visiting www.dorset-cc.gov.uk.

The Great West Dorset Cycle Ride, and 'Cycling Around' Leaflets: West Dorset District Council, Leisure and Tourism Division has produced a range of four inexpensive leaflets providing directions and sketch maps for cycling in its area. These can be obtained from either Dorchester, Bridport, Lyme Regis or Sherborne tourist information centres.

HAMPSHIRE

Off-Road Cycle Trails: The Hampshire County Council Countryside and Community Department has produced two off-road cycle packs, each containing 12 trail leaflets. The routes range from 2½ miles to 26 miles and use both quiet roads and the off-road right of way network. These are very well produced, waterproof, full-colour leaflets. However, the trails are most suitable for young and fit adults who are experienced cyclists and, except in a few cases, are not suitable for families with young children, as many of them are graded as strenuous. My recent experience is that the increasing prevalence of four-wheel drive vehicles and motorbikes on rights of way makes the ground heavy going, almost impassable in winter and very rutted in summer. The packs are available for a charge from some tourist information centres, or Countryside and Community Department, Mottisfont Court, High Street, Winchester, Hants SO23 8ZF (tel: 01962 846045). The council's website is at www.hants.gov.uk.

The Test Valley Tour: This is a series of 25 circular walking and cycling routes produced by Test Valley Borough Council. They can be bought as complete packs, or split into individual walking and cycling packs. They are available from local tourist information centres or from the council (tel: 01264 368833).

Discover East Hampshire Area of Outstanding Natural Beauty by Bike: Published by Hampshire County Council with assistance from East Hants District Council and Alton Cycling Club, this is a circular route of 22 miles from Petersfield through Hawkley, Froxfield Green and East Meon. This free leaflet is available from local tourist information centres or by contacting Hampshire County Council Recreational Cycling Officer (tel: 01962 846172), or East Hampshire AONB Officer (tel: 023 9259 1362).

THE NATIONAL CYCLE ROUTE

The completion of a National Cycle Network for Britain has been the aim of the charity Sustrans (**Sus**tainable **Trans**port) for 20 years and the project received a tremendous boost by obtaining funding of £42 million in 1995 from the Millennium Commission from National Lottery funds. Sustrans completed the first 5,000 miles in June 2000, with the remaining 4,000 miles due to be completed by 2005. Although the project is led by Sustrans, it is a partnership with over 400 local authorities and land-owning bodies, government departments and specialist and local interest groups. It will consist of approximately 50% traffic-free sections, with the remainder on segregated or traffic-calmed roads. A fundamental design aim is that the whole network will be safe for use by a sensible, unsupervised 12 year old.

The route through Hampshire and Dorset will consist of Main Route 2 that runs east/west from Havant to Lyme Regis following the south coast. There are also Routes 22, 23, 24, 25, 26 and 33 that radiate northwards from this south coast route to connect to other main routes of the network. At the time of writing, though, virtually none of the proposed route through Hampshire and Dorset has been completed, and so we must be patient over the next few years to realise the benefits of this enormous investment.

THE NATIONAL BYWAY

This is a 3,000-mile heritage cycling route around Britain that links many sites of interest and uses mainly quiet country lanes. It is being developed on a section by section basis and is supported by Hovis. I was surprised to learn that Hovis have been involved with cycling since 1899 when they first published a series of maps highlighting good cycling routes and also where to get a Hovis tea. The area of interest to this book is the 154-mile Winchester-Shaftesbury-Winchester section that links Winchester, Salisbury, Shaftesbury and Fordingbridge. The route is well waymarked (but in one direction only — anti-clockwise). (Tel: 01425 650166 to enquire about the inexpensive leaflet or for more information about the National Byway.)

Below:
The village well in East Marden.

Note: If a contact address or telephone is not shown for the publishing authority, you will find it in the 'Useful Addresses' chapter.

DORSET

Cycle Around South Somerset and West Dorset: A well-produced free leaflet covering an 80-mile cycle ride in the two counties, available from Tourism and Cultural Services, South Somerset District Council, Brympton Way, Yeovil, Somerset BA20 2HT (tel: 01935 462462; web: www.southsomerset.gov.uk).

The North Dorset Cycleway: This is a circular route of 73 miles with some linking routes that make shorter day rides possible. This free leaflet is available from local tourist information centres or by contacting Cycling, Environmental Services Directorate, County Hall, Dorchester, Dorset DT1 1XJ (tel: 01305 224558; web: www.dorset-cc.gov.uk).

The Purbeck Cycleway: This has a main circular route of 47 miles with two loops of 12 miles and one of 22 miles. A free leaflet is available from local tourist information centres or by contacting Cycling, Environmental Services Directorate, County Hall, Dorchester, Dorset DT1 1XJ (tel: 01305 224558; web: www.dorset-cc.gov.uk).

The Castleman Trailway: This route is for cyclists and walkers and runs for 16 miles from Upton Country Park near Poole to the River Avon at Ringwood. At present, it is only fully open to walkers, and cyclists have to seek an alternative route over the section from Dolman's Crossing to West Moors. Free leaflets are available from local tourist information centres or by contacting Dorset County Council's Countryside Service Eastern Offices (tel: 01425 478082; web: www.dorset-cc.gov.uk).

The Great West Dorset Cycle Ride, and 'Cycling Around' Leaflets: A range of four inexpensive leaflets produced by West Dorset District Council, Leisure and Tourism Division and available from Dorchester, Bridport, Lyme Regis or Sherborne tourist information centres.

Moors Valley Country Park Leaflet: This covers four short virtually traffic-free and waymarked cycle routes, 10 miles north of Bournemouth at Horton Road, Ashley Heath, Ringwood, Hants BH24 2ET. The free leaflet is available from the park (tel: 01425 470721 for Information Point and Wardens' Office).

Cycleways in Poole: Available from Poole Borough Council.

HAMPSHIRE

Off-Road Cycle Trails: Two off-road cycle packs, each containing 12 trail leaflets. The packs are available for a charge from some tourist information centres, or Countryside and Community Department, Mottisfont Court, High Street, Winchester, Hants SO23 8ZF (tel: 01962 846045; web: www.hants.gov.uk).

Along and Around the Wayfarers Walk: This includes two sections open to cyclists (Inkpen Beacon to North Oakley and Dummer to Hinton Ampner). Available from Countryside and Community Department, Mottisfont Court, High Street, Winchester, Hants SO23 8ZF (tel: 01962 846045; web: www.hants.gov.uk).

Queen Elizabeth Country Park, Trails Guide and Map: Obtainable for a small charge from Queen Elizabeth Country Park, Gravel Hill, Horndean, Hants PO8 0QE (Tel: 023 9259 5040).

The Test Valley Tour: A series of 25 circular walking and cycling route leaflets produced by Test Valley Borough Council. They can be bought as complete packs, or split into individual walking and cycling packs. They are available from local tourist information centres or from the council (tel: 01264 368833).

Discover East Hampshire Area of Outstanding Natural Beauty by Bike: A leaflet detailing a 22-mile circular route through Petersfield, Hawkley, Froxfield Green and East Meon. This free leaflet is available from local tourist information centres or by contacting Hampshire County Council Recreational Cycling Officer (tel: 01962 846172), or East Hampshire AONB Officer (tel: 023 9259 1362).

Alice Holt Woodland Park Leaflet: This covers the cycling opportunities on off-road trails and gravelled tracks in the park situated on the Hampshire/Surrey border just southwest of Farnham. It is available from the Forest Centre (tel: 07775 840807).

Cycling in the New Forest — The Network Map: This covers all of the gravelled tracks and most suitable roads in the New Forest and is available for a small charge from the Forestry Commission, the Queen's House, Lyndhurst, Hampshire SO43 7NH (tel: 023 8028 3141). It is also widely available from local tourist information centres, cycle hire shops, camp sites and other outlets in the area.

Basingstoke Cycleways: A free leaflet showing the main cycle routes in the borough. Available from Basingstoke & Deane Borough Council or Basingstoke area tourist information centres.

Eastleigh Cycleways Guide: A free leaflet available from Eastleigh Borough Council.

Portsmouth Cycle Routes: Two free leaflets showing the city's cycle routes. Available from Portsmouth City Council.

Southampton Cyclists Guide: A free leaflet available from Southampton City Council.

Winchester Cycle Routes: A free leaflet showing the main cycle routes in the city. Available from Winchester Tourist Information Centre.

HAMPSHIRE AND DORSET
The National Byway South West England Leaflet. An inexpensive leaflet covering the 154-mile section of the route that is situated in the southwest of England, and links Winchester, Salisbury, Shaftesbury and Fordingbridge. (Tel: 01425 650166 to enquire about the leaflet or for more information about the National Byway.)

USEFUL ADDRESSES

The county council is a good starting point to find out the local cycle routes in a particular area. Some lower level councils (district councils or unitary councils) are also involved with cycle route development to a varying degree and these are also listed below. The particular department that deals with cycling promotion varies from council to council. Often it is the technical services or similarly named department, but it can be economic development or tourism. For simplicity, I have quoted the 'technical' department as your starting point in each case.

County Councils

DORSET
Director of Environmental Services, Dorset County Council, County Hall, Colliton Park, Dorchester DT1 1XJ (tel: 01305 224216).

HAMPSHIRE
The County Surveyor, Hampshire County Council, The Castle, Winchester SO23 8UD (tel: 01962 847055).

District and Unitary Councils

CHRISTCHURCH
Director of Leisure and Technical Services, Christchurch Borough Council, Civic Offices, Bridge Street, Christchurch BH23 1AZ (tel: 01202 495000).

EAST DORSET
District Environmental Services Officer, East Dorset District Council, Council Offices, Furze Hill, Wimborne, BH21 4HN (tel: 01202 886201).

EASTLEIGH
Head of Engineering, Eastleigh Borough Council, Civic Offices, Leigh Road, Eastleigh SO50 9YN (tel: 023 8062 2238; web: www.eastleigh.gov.uk).

FAREHAM
Strategic Director of Planning and Development, Fareham Council, PO Box 82, Civic Offices, Civic Way, Fareham PO16 7TT (tel: 01329 236100).

GOSPORT
Development Services Manager, Gosport Borough Council, Town Hall, Gosport PO12 1EB (tel: 023 9254 5409; web: www.gosport.gov.uk)

HART
Head of Technical Services, Hart District Council, Civic Offices, Harlington Way, Fleet GU13 8AE (tel: 01252 774425; web: www.hart.gov.uk/hartdc).

HAVANT
Head of Technical Services, Havant Borough Council, Civic Offices, Civic Centre Road, Havant PO9 2AX (tel: 023 9244 6400; web: www.havant.gov.uk).

NEW FOREST
Director of Environment Services, New Forest District Council, Town Hall, Avenue Road, Lymington SO41 9ZG (tel: 023 8028 5603).

NORTH DORSET
Head of Technical Services, North Dorset District Council, Nordon, Salisbury Road, Blandford Forum DT11 7LL (tel: 01258 454111).

POOLE
Highways Department, Poole Borough Council, Civic Centre, Poole BH15 2RU (tel: 01202 633249).

PORTSMOUTH
City Engineer, Portsmouth City Council, Civic Offices, Guildhall Square, Portsmouth PO1 2AS (tel 023 9283 4573).

RUSHMOOR
Director of Environmental Services, Rushmoor Borough Council, Council Offices, Farnborough Road, Farnborough GU14 7JU (tel: 01252 398398; web: www.rushmoor.gov.uk).

SOUTHAMPTON
Development Policy & Planning Division, Marland House, Civic Centre Road, Southampton SO14 7PQ (tel: 023 8022 3855).

TEST VALLEY
Head of Technical Services, Test Valley Borough Council, Beechurst, Wey Hill Road, Andover SP10 3AJ (tel: 01264 364144; web: www.testvalley.gov.uk).

WEST DORSET
Engineering Manager, West Dorset District Council, Stratton House, 58-60, High West Street, Dorchester DT1 1UZ (tel: 01305 251010).

WEYMOUTH AND PORTLAND
Borough Engineer, Weymouth & Portland Borough Council, Municipal Offices, North Quay, Weymouth DT4 8TA (tel: 01305 206299; web: www.weymouth.gov.uk).

WINCHESTER
Chief Engineer, Winchester City Council, City Offices, Colebrook Street, Winchester SO23 9LJ (tel: 01962 840222).

Tourist Information Centres

ALDERSHOT
Military Museum, Queens Avenue, Aldershot, Hants GU11 2LG (tel: 01252 320968).

ALTON
7 Cross and Pillory Lane, Alton, Hampshire GU34 1HL (tel: 01420 88448).

ANDOVER
Town Mill House, Bridge Street, Andover, Hampshire SP10 1BL (tel: 01264 324320).

BASINGSTOKE
Willis Museum, Old Town Hall, Market Place, Basingstoke, Hampshire RG21 7QD (tel: 01256 817618).

BRIDPORT
32 South Street, Bridport, Dorset DT6 3NQ (tel: 01308 424901).

BLANDFORD FORUM
Marsh and Ham Car Park, West Street, Blandford Forum, Dorset DT11 7HD (tel: 01258 454770).

BOURNEMOUTH
Westover Road, Bournemouth, Dorset BH1 2BU (tel: 01202 451700).

BRIDPORT
32 South Street, Bridport, Dorset DT6 3NQ (tel: 01308 424901).

CHRISTCHURCH
23 High Street, Christchurch, Dorset BH23 1AB (tel: 01202 471780).

DORCHESTER
Unit 11, Antelope Walk, Dorchester, Dorset DT1 1BE (tel: 01305 267992).

EASTLEIGH
The Point, Leigh Road, Eastleigh, Hampshire SO50 9DE (tel: 023 8064 1261).

FAREHAM
Westbury Manor, West Street, Fareham, Hampshire PO16 OJJ (tel: 01329 221342).

FLEET
The Harlington Centre, 236 Fleet Road, Fleet, Hampshire GU13 8BY (tel: 01252 811151).

FORDINGBRIDGE
(Open Easter to September only) Kings Yard, Salisbury Street, Fordingbridge, Hampshire SP6 1AB (tel: 01425 654560).

GOSPORT
1 High Street, Gosport, Hampshire PO12 1BX (tel: 023 9252 2944).

HAVANT
1 Park Road South, Havant, Hampshire PO9 1HA (tel: 023 9248 0024).

LYME REGIS
Guildhall Cottage, Church Street, Lyme Regis, Dorset DT7 3BS (tel: 01297 442138).

LYMINGTON
St Barb Museum and Visitor Centre, New Street, Lymington, Hampshire SO41 9BH (tel: 01590 672422).

NEW FOREST
New Forest Museum and Visitor Centre, Main Car Park, Lyndhurst, Hampshire SO43 7NY (tel: 023 8028 2269).

PETERSFIELD
The County Library, 27 The Square, Petersfield, Hampshire GU32 3HH (tel: 01730 268829).

POOLE
The Quay, Poole, Dorset BH15 1HE (tel: 01202 253253).

PORTSMOUTH
The Hard, Portsmouth, Hampshire PO1 3QJ (tel: 023 9282 6722).

PURBECK
Purbeck Information and Heritage Centre, South Street, Wareham, Dorset BH20 4LU (tel: 01929 552740).

RINGWOOD
The Furlong, Ringwood, Hampshire BH24 1AZ (tel: 01425 470896).

ROMSEY
1 Latimer Street, Romsey, Hampshire SO51 8DF (tel: 01794 512987).

SHERBORNE
3 Tilton Court, Digby Road, Sherborne, Dorset DT9 3NL (tel: 01935 815341).

SOUTHAMPTON
9 Civic Centre Road, Southampton, Hampshire SO14 7LP (tel: 023 8022 1106).

SWANAGE
The White House, Shore Road, Swanage, Dorset BH19 1LB (tel: 01929 422885).

WEYMOUTH
The King's Statue, The Esplanade, Weymouth, Dorset DT4 7AN (tel: 01305 785747).

WIMBORNE MINSTER
29 High Street, Wimborne Minster, Dorset BH21 1HR (tel: 01202 886116).

WINCHESTER
Guildhall, The Broadway, Winchester, Hampshire SO23 9LJ (tel: 01962 840500).

Other Organisations

CYCLISTS TOURING CLUB (CTC)
Cotterell House, 69 Meadrow, Godalming, Surrey GU7 3HS (tel: 01483 417217; web: www.ctc.org.uk). The CTC is Britain's national cyclists' association and works for all cyclists. It provides advice, legal aid and insurance, and campaigns to improve facilities and opportunities for cyclists. It publishes a very useful guide to the cycle routes in England, Wales, Scotland and Ireland and a directory of cycle hire outlets.

SUSTRANS
35 King Street, Bristol BS1 4DZ (tel: 0117 926 8893; web: www.sustrans.org.uk). Sustrans is a national charity that designs and builds traffic-free routes for cyclists, pedestrians and disabled people. It is promoting the National Cycle Network that will comprise over 6,500 miles in the four home countries, and is scheduled to be completed by 2005.

THE NATIONAL BYWAY
PO Box 128, Newark, Nottinghamshire NG23 6BL (tel: 01636 636818).

FORESTRY COMMISSION
SE England Forest District, Bucks Horn Oak, Wrecclesham, Farnham Surrey GU10 4LS (tel: 01420 23666; web: www.forestry.gov.uk)

New Forest District, The Queen's House, Lyndhurst, Hampshire SO43 7NH (tel: 023 8028 3929).

New Forest Cycle Hire Outlets:

Such is the scope for cycling in the New Forest that there are many more cycle hire outlets than in the remainder of the two counties. This list, although it may not be completely comprehensive, includes all that I was able to locate.

AA BIKE HIRE
Fern Glen, Gosport Lane, Lyndhurst (tel: 023 8028 3349).

ADVENTURE CYCLE HIRE — BASHLEY PARK
Bashley Park, Sway Road (B3055), New Milton (tel: 01425 615593).

ADVENTURE CYCLE HIRE — BEAULIEU
Adjacent to motor museum (B3056), Beaulieu (tel: 01425 615593).

ASHLEY CYCLES
49 Ashley Road, New Milton (tel: 01425 618103).

BALMER LAWN BIKE HIRE,
Balmer Lawn Road, Brockenhurst (tel: 01590 622181).

BURLEY BIKE HIRE,
Village Centre, Burley (tel: 01425 403584).

COUNTRY LANES CYCLE CENTRE
Sandy Balls Estate, Godshill, Fordingbridge (tel: 01425 657707; web: www.countrylanes.co.uk).

COUNTRY LANES CYCLE CENTRE
The Railway Carriage, Brockenhurst Station, Brockenhurst (tel: 01590 622627; web: www.countrylanes.co.uk).

NEW FOREST CYCLE EXPERIENCE
Island Shop, Brookley Road, Brockenhurst (tel: 01590 624204; web: www.bikeshop.demon.co.uk).

PERKINS
7 Provost Street, Fordingbridge (tel: 01425 653475).

RENT A BIKE
56 Brookley Road. Brockenhurst (tel: 01590 681876).

Below: Beaulieu. Peter Titmuss/ Southern Tourist Board